CW01494999

1

I dedicate this book to my partner in life, Dean Gibson, whose unwavering love, kindness and dedication through the many highs and lows allow me to be here today.

Bill Sydnor

3

Living Day by Day With MSA

Journeying Through Life With A Diagnosis of Multiple System Atrophy

Bill Sydnor

Fort Lauderdale, Florida

The Beginning-

In the Spring 2010, during an annual physical, my physician of many years, Charles Stinson, asked, "How long have you been dragging that left dragging leg?"

"Am I dragging it?" I asked. "I haven't really noticed. I think I'm just tired. Pushing myself too hard lately." At the time, I was overseeing a program for homeless school-aged youth in one of the largest school districts in the United States. It was a daunting task.

"You seem to have some neuropathy in your feet, especially you're left. Hold out your arms, palms up." I did so. Both my hands shook loosely. "Can you control that?" I replied that I couldn't.

Dr. Stinson then began to test my reflexes. "Hyper reflexive," he noted. He tracked my eyes. "Are you having any trouble reading?"

"Yes, a bit. My eyes fatigue easily."

"It appears that the tracking is off," he stated as he continued his assessment. "Any trouble with sexual performance? Erection problems?"

"Well..." I resisted. "Yes, but as I said, I'm just worn out these days."

He listened to my chest. "Any trouble breathing?"

"Sometimes."

"Urgency urinating?"

"At times. What's going on?" I asked.

"Some things are a bit off," Dr. Stinson replied. "I'm not sure why, but I'm going to refer you to a neurologist."

"What?" I answered in surprise. "A neurologist? No, no, I'm fine. I told you, my job is just really stressful."

"He'll want to do some tests. Just to rule things out." he handed me a referral. I looked at it with shock and confusion. I was expecting a simple physical, which I always flew through with barely a comment. "Try to contact him this week. He'll do some tests and send me his findings. We'll go from there. I might just be overly cautious."

"Okay," I replied as I gathered up my things. "Let's hope so!" Dr. Stinson and I shook hands and I became lost in thought as I made my way to my car. "What in the world is he thinking?" I wondered.

Soon I would find out.

Dr. Stinson's referral was to a neurologist just out of town. My partner, Dean, accompanied me to the appointment, which consisted of a basic assessment.

"I'm going to suggest a CT scan and an MRI," he summarized. "There is something going on here, but we need more information.

"Something like Parkinson's? Or MS?" I asked.

"I don't think so," he replied. "Let's get these scans done and see what we're dealing with."

More mystery lied ahead. The CT scan and MRI revealed nothing to the neurologist, who surmised that a spinal stenosis might have been the cause.

"Have you been involved in any car accidents? Falls?" he inquired. I explained that yes, I had. He ordered an MRI of the spine, top to bottom. Within a month, we were back in his office to discuss the results.

"There appears to be a cervical stenosis that could easily cause your symptoms," he explained. "We can correct these surgically." He then began to describe the process in rather frightening detail. "I work with a very good neurosurgeon; he has years of experience doing this procedure. Make an appointment to consult with him."

A month or so later, Dean and I sat in the neurosurgeon's office. I was extremely nervous, for good reason it turns out. He ordered a lumbar puncture (spinal tap) to examine the fluid that surrounds the brain and spinal cord. It's called a lumbar puncture because a needle is placed in the lumbar portion of the back and punctures tissues to enter the spinal canal.

Might I suggest that no one undergo this procedure unless it is an absolute necessity for treatment. The pain during the operation was nearly unbearable; the pain afterwards left me nearly crippled. I was admitted to the hospital to determine why I was so debilitated. It was determined that the puncture had not sealed after the procedure, resulting in a spinal fluid leak. This caused an imbalance in spinal fluid pressure. Fortunately, this situation healed itself during my hospital stay, staving off a corrective procedure involving another puncture. The thought of that brought me to tears.

Many weeks later, a follow-up consultation with the neurosurgeon brought an unexpected conclusion. No surgery. He saw nothing in all the tests that would result in my presenting symptoms. He suggested that the neurologist(s) keep looking.

My physician, Dr. Stinson, suggested we start consulting new neurologists to seek their opinions. A local hospital was well known for their Department of Neurology; I was able to meet with the department head. He reviewed all my scans, tests and assessments and then performed a few of his own.

"There are definite signs of neurological disease. May I send your records to Mayo Clinic for records review?"

"Of course," I replied. "What might it be?"

"I'm not yet in a position to answer that," he replied.

By this point, we were entering 2011.

The new year brought bitter news. The Department of Neurology at Mayo Clinic had, in their review of my records, confirmed my neurologist's suspicions – multiple system atrophy. I had never heard of it. So many questions.

"Is it like MS? Parkinson's? How did this happen? Is it genetic?" And, of course," how is it treated?" I wasn't comforted by the answers.

"Sadly, this is a degenerative disease. There is no effective treatment, no cure at this time."

"Okay…how long will I live?"

"It's hard to tell. The average life expectancy after diagnosis is 8 years. Some patients live longer."

"I really want to know your opinion," I insisted. "I do better knowing what I'm up against. What do you think in my case?"

He looked me directly in the eye. "Given your symptoms and rate of progression, I'd say 66-72 months." Tears ran down Dean's face.

"I'll prove you wrong." I replied firmly, with a smile.

"I hope you do. Now, I do have something to offer you," the neurologist added. "A clinical trial will start this fall for Rifampin. Mayo Clinic would like you to be a part of it."

"Do you think I should?" I queried.

"I can't say. It's your decision. If it were me, I would do it, though. Rifampin is FDA-approved for other uses. Therefore, the risks are lower." He shared with me information about Rifampin and the links to the National Institutes of Health clinical trials site. "There will only be 100 participants. Think it over." I did just that.

For the next 9 years, I shared nearly all of my MSA adventures on Facebook. I created a page, Living Day By Day With MSA.

Here is where my journal began –

2010

September 10, 2010

Today was not was very restful! For those of you following the saga, some rot is affecting my legs. I fell Wednesday morning as I got ready for work, hit my head and was knocked out for 3 hours! Frontal lobe concussion - so, 2 days in the hospital for scans, tests and yada yada! Egad!

September 13, 2010

Well, 5 neuro evals in 2.5 weeks is a bit much…darn it!

September 22, 2010

Bill's Not So Excellent NeuroAdventure: Neurosurgeon wants an analysis of spinal fluid to rule out organic causes contributing to my condition before proceeding with surgery . Yes, this is good and throrough - but madding all the same. Thanks for all you kind and supportive notes!

October 4, 2020

Bill's Not So Excellent NeuroAdventure: not so excellent -surgery postoned, med records going to Mayo for review/opinion, everything on hold -

October 10, 2010

So, sometime last night, in the wee hours, my left leg must have told my right leg to quit working so hard. "Take it easy. Relax." Apparently, my legs have formed a Labor Union. I hope that negotiations are possible!

November 12, 2010

…if (a=b), and (b=c), then (a=c). And if $a(b+c) = ab+ac$, then why won't my damned legs move when I want them to!?

seek illumination wherever you may find it

dataMSA.com

2011

March 14, 2011

March is Multiple System Atrophy Awareness Month- approximately 50,000 Americans suffer from multiple system atrophy. Strong need exists for more awareness and education regarding diagnosis and management of this rare disease. Currently there is no cure or effective way to slow the progression of MSA and funding for more research is desperately required.

June 13, 2011

'Bill's Not-So-Excellent Neuro Adventure' Update: Doctor reports that the MSA is progressing, but slowly and that I am adjusting to it and doing better (no falls, etc.). He put me on a

Parkinson's med to reduce tremors - which may or may not work. Also, he states that I can be a little more flexible with the MS diet I am on. I see him again in 3 months, unless there are significant changes. That's all for now!

September 9, 2011

Here's the update: I go to Mayo/JAX for tests/assessment on 10/10 at 10am (for most of the day) ... with further work on 10/13.... then home for a while, taking clinical meds ... then back to Mayo 3x within a year... with monthly follow up with my neuro team here. Fingers, toes and eyes crossed! Thanks for all your kind words...

December 27, 2011

Could it be? Could it be, dare I ask.... could these meds slowly be bringing change?! It may be like turning the Titanic...but there is hope! "hard to port, full astern."

2012

February 9, 2012

Hello, all. I am a 54 y/o (m) MSA patient in FL who is part of the FDA MSA Clinical Trial under the auspices of Mayo Clinic - I am at the 6-month point of the 1yr study. I was diagnosed 18 months ago and have experienced a rather steady deterioration in mental and physical abilities for the past 3 years or more.

I am grateful for a well-informed neuro team here and at Mayo and remain hopeful for a brighter tomorrow! I do hope that the Clinical Trials prove helpful for all of us.

December 18, 2012

On a few occasions, "I've fallen, and I can't get up!" As much as I hate to admit it, and as much as I have put it off, I think it's time for a Life Alert-or something. Anyone out there have any experience with these doo-hickies?

Mar 26, 2012

I was diagnosed with MSA about 1.5 years ago. It took a team of doctors several months to determine the diagnosis...a process of elimination! For the past 5.5 months, I have participated in an FDA clinical trial for Rifampicin, under the auspices of Mayo clinic.

, it sems the effects of the meds may have leveled off. 2 months, I have been on a plateau. Not getting orse, not seeing improvement.

However, the illness has spread into my eyes - both optic nerves are damaged. I have very high light sensitivity and trouble focusing for any length of time. I spend hours each day 'resting my eyes' and listening to TV or radio. Today was no exception.

April 1, 2012

Had breakfast yesterday with a friend who suffers from Alzheimer's Disease. Like many of us with MSA, his blood pressure fluctuates easily. He took a tumble and broke his nose! Good reminder for me to go slow when I stand up!

April 5, 2012

One of the most peculiar effects of my MSA symptoms is the increased intensity of synesthesia, which I've experiences since childhood. My senses become crossed. I 'see' sound as light and color. I also 'see' touch. Taking a shower this morning was like an intense fireworks show in my mind's eye! Does anyone else experience this? Fascinating, but exhausting!

April 8, 2012

Next week, I consult with my neurologist, then a trip back to Mayo JAX on the 19th. I am eager to learn what positive effects the trial meds are having. Then, 6 more months!

Apr 9, 2012

Had a very solid night's sleep last night, which I really needed. My neurologist suggested marijuana in baked goods an hour before bed to aide with REM cycle sleep. One fourth of a brownie does the trick. BTW: I must be the only child of the 70s who never touched the stuff before...

Apr 15, 2012

Neurology appt tomorrow morning, before I head up to Mayo later in the week. Eager to learn what he 'sees'... I have so many questions for him and my Mayo doctors. Some things seem better, but I feel like I have 'aged' so much in this past

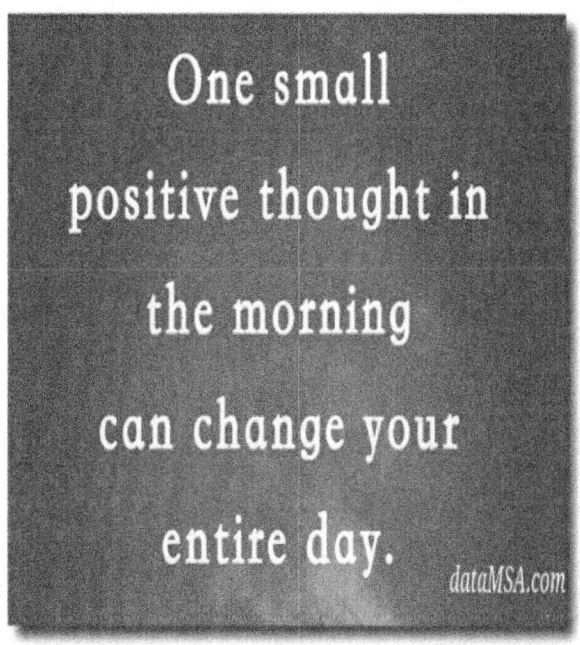

year. As long as I can keep my spirit afloat, I think I'll be OK!

April 16, 2012

Recv'd a pretty good report from my neurologist this morning... it appears that the trial drugs are doing something positive! I will know more after my trip to Mayo this week. Fingers crossed - and eyes and toes and ......

April 17, 2012

I am so grateful to be a part of the Rifampicin clinical trial. The first 3 months were very challenging (oh brother!), but here at the 6 month point, my neurologist sees improvement… and so do I. Day after tomorrow, I head back up to Mayo Clinic for my 50,000-mile checkup. I am optimistic and always hopeful!

Apr 21, 2012

Good news from Mayo Clinic. It appears that none of my symptoms have worsened in the past 6 months...most are unchanged, and a few may have improved! Fan-frakkin-tastic!

April 23, 2012

Great to be back home again. The trip to Mayo Clinic JAX was uplifting and one of healing and hope. I learned that the clinical drugs may indeed be doing something positive. My trial period ends in October, when I will return to Mayo for the final study visit. If the trends continue, I will be one very lucky man.

For those who may not have been able to participate in this particular study, do speak with your neuro team about the Rifampicin FDA study and learn if you may be able to receive the drug locally, even prior to FDA approval for MSA (it is already approved for other usages). Mayo neuros report that this medication may be our greatest hope!

April 24, 2012

Just an FYI: I asked the neuro team at Mayo Clinic about the long- term effects of Rifampicin. They report that there is little risk for long-term damage, but that the liver must be monitored through regular blood labs. They also report that, at times, patients may take a 'rest' from the meds, if there are issues. Do remember that the side effects are powerful. For me they lasted for 3.5 months - but it was worth coming out the other side of them. Some of the national clinical trial participants dropped out because of the harsh effects... luckily for me, all those rotten side issues have passed. Chin up!

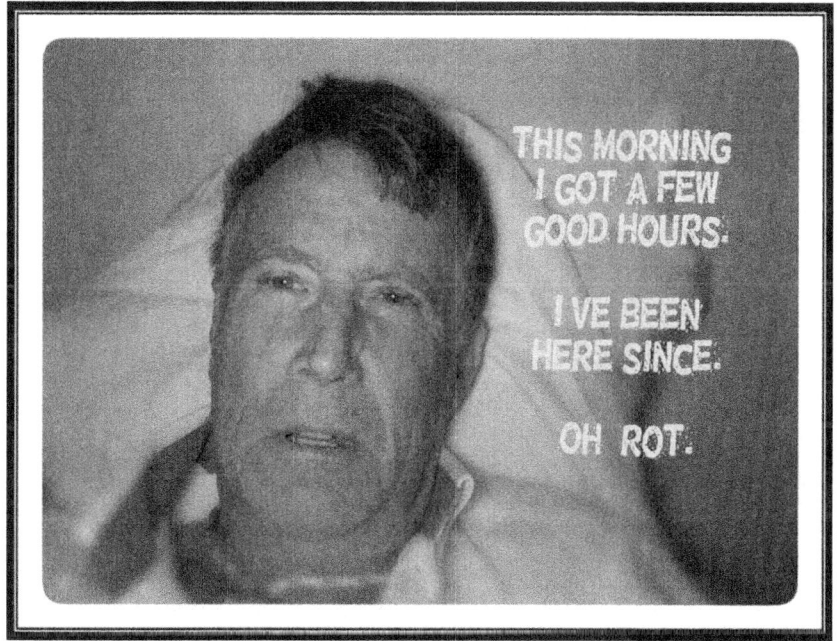

April 25, 2012

It seems that all the events at Mayo Clinic finally caught up with me! I spent the past few days feeling totally exhausted and weak. I have pulled up and out of it a bit this evening. Again, energy comes to me in units and if I expend too much too fast, I face exhaustion and worsening of some symptoms. Moderation... a concept I am slow to grasp!

April 30, 2012

Do others find that their MSA symptoms cycle in severity? I am finally coming out of a 2.5-day funk with lots of rot and low ability. I have tried to record these episodes to determine cause, but nothing seems to make sense.

not all MSA symptoms are on the surface

dataMSA.com

© Renee Capozzola

May 1, 2012

Oh, good grief. Today, I worked up enough energy to go to the wellness center to do some sort of light work-out. I signed up a year ago, but my condition had grown so much worse that I never went. Finally, today was the day! But it's on the 8th floor of a large labyrinth of a hospital and I became lost. By the time I found it, I was too exhausted to do anything and barely made it back to the car. Tomorrow is another day...

May 9, 2012

"Bill's Not-So Excellent Neuro Adventure" Word of the Day: Synesthesia -a neurological condition in which stimulation of one sensory or cognitive pathway leads to automatic, involuntary experiences in a second sensory or cognitive pathway. It makes me feel as if I am losing my mind...oh wait, that may be what's causing it!

May 16, 2012

Wrapping up Month 7 of the one-year clinical Rifampicin Trial. Still experiencing some strong side effects, including upper/lower GI discomfort and chronic fatigue. However, the worst has passed, and I hold fast that I have benefitted from this trial. Always hopeful for a better tomorrow!

May 18, 2012

I have to budget my energy like one would budget money. Yesterday, I spent too much and today I am 'broke' . . . but, it was worth it!

June 2, 2012

Closing this page for a while and staying off support pages... I realize I was surrendering too much energy to the rot of MSA. Time to upshift to more (+) thoughts... Overdrive!

June 8, 2012

By 9th grade, I deeply disliked public school. By 10th grade, due to violence and poor leadership, I grew to hate it. By 12th grade, I had dropped out. Now, due to MSA, I close 24 years as a public-school educator. I hope I made a few things better for our youth….

I would suggest you discuss these options with your health care providers, PT/OT and neurologist(s) to reduce any risks of harm.

If you'd like more information about the techniques I employee, drop me a line. I follow studies on neuro training, redundant circuits and brain plasticity. I think it's helping, but at least it makes me feel I'm doing something positive for myself.

July 12, 2012

Today was a pretty fine day! I was able to do some volunteer work and met a friend for a wee lunch out . . . I am always grateful for days like this! More, please!

July 15, 2012

The Gifts of MSA:

1) learning to live in the moment, moment by moment by moment

2) being able to focus on what truly matters and discarding what doesn't

3) accepting love and compassion...and help now and then!

4) knowing that the road ahead will be OK... even if the map is confusing

5) accepting that life is a series of transitions and mortality is nothing to fear.

August 1, 2012

Had a therapy session today and talked about the adjustments and accommodations I must make to face MSA head-on... it helps to voice the frustrations ...

August 2, 2012

Setting my appointments for the conclusion of this Rifampicin clinical trial. My period ends in early October, although other participants had a later start date. I hope the docs and FDA find this drug effective and release it for MSA patients. It appears to be our only hope in slowing progression and extending quality of life, but there is still no cure at this point . . . fingers crossed

August 13, 2012

I've asked all my doctors if past blunt head trauma can contribute to MSA... 'cause I got whacked a few times doing this!

August 13, 2012

I call them 'lost days'... like today, when I was stuck in bed for 9-10 hours. But maybe they're not lost at all . . .. I hope they are actually 'healing days'!

The wind lifts my spirit. The sea calls me to carry on. I am indeed a lucky man.

dataMSA.com

August 14, 2012

Today was a fine day, with a lovely 2.5-hour nap. Such a difference from yesterday! I do wish it was cooler outside. I overheat so easily, even though I have lived in South Florida for 45 years! But I am thankful for a good day and hope for another one tomorrow! Hope is the key...

August 16, 2012

My sleep cycle is often a mess. Some nights, I get no sleep at all - up all night. Sometimes, I get sleep in 2-3-hour clips. I have tried all the recommended supplements through the years, and the only thing that works - really works consistently - is cannabis. I eat 1/2 a brownie about 1 hour before I intend to sleep, and it allows me several hours of uninterrupted rest. Works for me...maybe it may work for you, too. Rest is critical for us MSA folk!

August 22, 2012

...had a therapy session this morning, which helped me face the ongoing challenges and changes that MSA brings. I surely can't do what I used to do...but, it's more important that I focus on what I can do - and build on that!

August 27, 2012

Been struggling for a while with upper/lower GI discomfort. Dr. says long term use of Rifampicin has damaged the 'good' biotics, and recommended Florajen 3, 1x a day. I'll let you know if it works.... hope so!

September 16, 2012

One month to go in the FDA MSA Clinical Trial for Rifampicin. But what comes afterwards? My local neuro team plans to continue but perhaps adjust the dosage... and we must find a way to minimize some of the stronger side effects if I am to keep going. Overall, though, I am much better off than I was expected to be 2 years ago! The prognosis then was so grim... but, I may have beaten the odds (so far) Hooray!

September 22, 2012

The gifts of MSA: Stop fighting what can't be fought. Choose your battles. Sounds like a summary of life in general - if only I had learned this 40 years ago! Damned ego!

September 23, 2012

Whew - wicked couple of days. In bed useless. And the GI discomfort rocks me. Walking, eating, swallowing is difficult as

Hell. Breathing labored. Depression is poking at me. Gotta get back on track - a new dawn.

October 5, 2012

Bill's Not-So Excellent Neuro Adventure Update: Had a quarterly neuro eval yesterday with local doctors. My gate has worsened; I must use my cane to prevent falls (I have tried to not use it as much lately). Also, outcomes from Mayo Clinic visit in 2 weeks will determine future use/dosage of Rifampicin. Good news from primary doctor: the meds have not damaged my GI or other systems - all my discomfort will be treated with probiotics or other supplements. Hope it all works! More later...

November 12, 2012

Greetings, everyone. It's been awhile since I posted to this page - Last month, I completed the one-year, double-blind FDA Clinical Trial for Rifampicin through Mayo Clinic, Jacksonville. Both the research team and my local neurology team observed many side effects of the medication, BUT saw positive effects - particularly the retardation of disease progression.

However, my cognitive processing showed signs of worsening, and my gross and fine motor skills may have worsened a bit, as well. After one year, my autonomic systems showed no deterioration, with indications of slight improvement.

Last week, the study was aborted when each participant had reached or surpassed the 6-month point (we all started at different times). It was felt that the medication DID NOT positively impact the disease in the participants who were known to have taken the drug (and not a placebo).

Because the data did not indicate significant improvement, use of Rifampicin will NOT be considered an effective treatment for MSA. However, my experience differs. It has now been nearly five weeks since my last dose and, in this past week, I have seen some signs of regression.

Therefore, I plan to continue use of the drug, under the auspices of my local neurologist. We may adjust dosage to

MSA days are like fingerprints.
No two are exactly alike...

minimize challenging side effects. Stay tuned - it should be interesting! My best to each of you –

November 18, 2012

'Please, sir, I want some more. Some more Magic Beans.'

'What!' said the doctors at length, in a faint voice.

'Please, sir,' replied Bill, 'I want some more.'

'Mr. Doctors, I beg your pardon, sirs! Bill has asked for more Magic Beans!' There was a general start.

'For MORE!?' said Mr. Doctors. 'Do I understand that he asked for more, after he had taken all the Magic Beans allotted by the study?'

'He did, sir.'

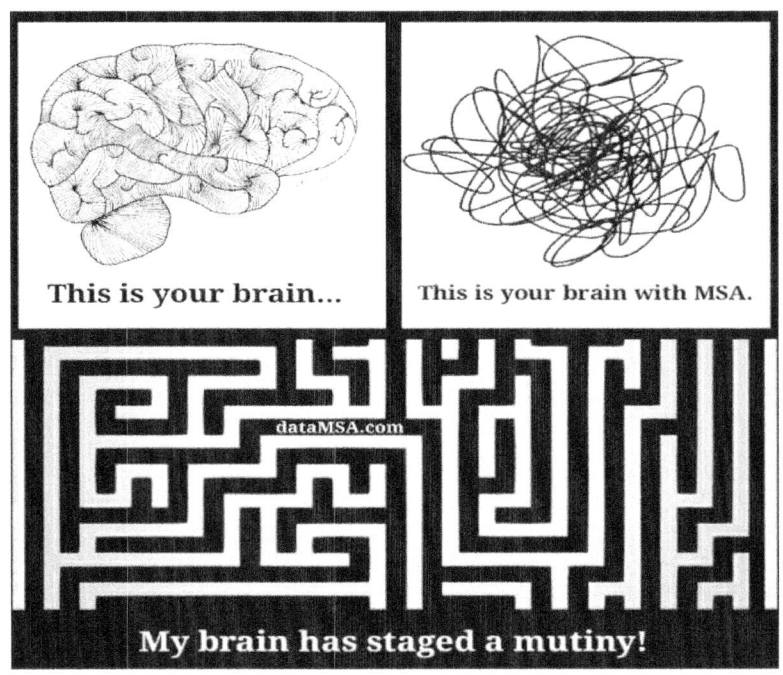

November 20, 2012

Whew! I seem to be on an upswing for the past 2 days! Oh, JOY! Have an appointment with my neurologist soon to discuss future treatment planning - but, for today, I am grateful to be up and about! Joy, oh Joy!

Dec 6, 2012

MSA is seen as something rather terrible to face - and it is. But, typically I choose to look at it from the 'dark cloud/silver lining' perspective. Because of MSA, I am better able to sort through what matters and what doesn't . . . who matters and who doesn't. I approach each day with hope, with no expectations

other than living in the moment. I take time for each challenge and celebrate each success. Maybe it's based on a childlike innocence- but that's ok with me! Like a child, I really don't worry much about tomorrow!

December 17, 2012

A good half bubble off plumb. Slept a lot today- not much last night. I had about 2 good hours this morning before my darned self went on strike for better conditions. Tomorrow will be better...I have learned to adapt and accept.

December 19, 2012

I love to sleep - but I'd rather sleep more at night and less during the day! Is this due to this MSA rot or simply just getting older?

2013

February 4, 2013

What an incredibly fine day here in South Florida! I got up and out for a brief walk on the beach. I stumbled and fell at times, but that's ok! Our sand is soft, warm, and smells good. The other day, while I was walking at the shoreline, local police stopped me, thinking I was intoxicated... because I look like I am. HA! Life is a hoot sometimes...

February 11, 2013

It may be easy to see the outward symptoms of MSA - an awkward gait, tremors, effects of absolute exhaustion. But, hidden deeper are effects of MSA that only the sufferer may see - trouble with breathing, eating, swallowing, toileting - failure of vision, of memory, of clear thought - anxiety, depression, and unmitigated fear that haunts dark moments.

It's a difficult illness to understand, but I try to keep the brightside up, facing the sunlight.

February 14, 2013

EUS National Library of Medicine, National Institutes of Health: Effects of caffeine in Parkinson's disease: from neuroprotection to the management of motor and non-motor symptoms.

"Nowadays there is considerable evidence showing that non-dopaminergic degeneration also occurs in other brain areas, emotional and memory functions that precede the classical motor symptoms in PD. The present review attempts to examine results reported in epidemiological, clinical and animal studies to provide a comprehensive picture of the antiparkinsonian potential of caffeine. Convergent epidemiological and pre-clinical data suggest that caffeine may confer neuroprotection against the underlying dopaminergic neuron degeneration, and influence the onset and progression of PD. The available data also suggest that caffeine can improve the motor deficits of PD and that adenosine A2A receptor antagonists such as istradefylline reduces OFF time and dyskinesia associated with standard 'dopamine replacement' treatments.

Finally, recent experimental findings have indicated the potential of caffeine in the management of non-motor symptoms of PD, which do not improve with the current dopaminergic drugs. Altogether, the studies reviewed provide strong evidence that caffeine may represent a promising therapeutic tool in PD, thus being the first compound to restore both motor and non-motor early symptoms of PD together with its neuroprotective potential."

February 16, 2013

Don't you hate it when: MSA has you lying flat on your back in the middle of the night. And your legs and feet are so numb, you aren't sure they're there. You're pretty sure they are, but it's dark, so you can't be quite sure. Maybe they fell off and are on the floor. Oh well. And you want to roll onto your side because the TV remote is jabbing you in the kidney. But your arms- well, they are plumb useless. So, you contort your torso and finally get flipped. But now your useless arm is in the way.

34

And when you eventually do get settled, and your breathing recovers, you suddenly become oddly aware of your tongue. Did it get bigger or something? Damn thing feels huge! Oh crap. And you try not to think about it. But it's just 'there'! Don't you just hate it?

February 19, 2013

I want to share information I learned today from Mayo Clinic, the preliminary results are in from the recent (and aborted) Rifampicin clinical trial. Data indicate those patients who received Rifamipicin actually did worse than did their colleagues on the placebo. Yes, worse. Rifampicin appears to have accelerated, rather than slowed, the progression of MSA in the participating individuals.

I inquired if there was any hope in adjusting dosage, etc. for better outcomes. At this time, the answer is negative. I further inquired if other clinical trials are on the near horizon regarding potential slowing of MSA progression. The answer was negative. But I am hopeful that just around the next corner . . .

February 27, 2013

Well, I had a fine consultation with my neurologists yesterday. They discussed the Rifampicin trial outcomes and shared that the overall results were very poor (which I knew from my Mayo Clinic doctors). So, no go there. If any of you are currently taking Rifampicin, you may want to discuss these outcomes with your doctors. We also discussed the 'intravenous immunoglobulin' studies. These studies have demonstrated good outcomes, but the effects are short-lived (6 months+/-) and the treatment is terribly expensive (10K+/-). However, as these studies progress (mostly with Alzheimer's patients at this point), they offer much hope to many.

And, as Martha Stewart would say - "That's a good thing".

March 6, 2013

Had an appointment with my general practitioner this morning...his father suffered with MSA for 7 years and passed last December. Because of his family experiences, he is able to gently guide me through each transition - and I am grateful for his knowledge.

When I presented unusual symptoms, it was he who referred me to some of the top specialists in South Florida. Today, with kindness in his eyes, he said, "Never stop smiling. Never become so overwhelmed that you lose out on the day." Then, he added, "That's the greatest lesson I learned from my father." Hats off to all the folks out there who take good care of us!

In order to test my limits...

I have to take a few risks.

March 13, 2013

My personal MSA Awareness tips:

a) Stay hydrated throughout the day. Constant hydration is critical for effective neuro functioning- as well as overall system functioning.

b) MSA often causes both emotional AND chemical depression. Antidepression medication may elevate mood and positively effect cognitive functioning. However, all medication has a 'window of effectiveness' - dosing too low may do nothing; dosing too high can create adverse effects. MSA often shifts the 'recommended' dosage - so, communicate with doctors often to ensure proper levels.

c) Once-a-day multivitamins are likely not enough. Lab work can detect deficiencies that require attention. Low vitamin D levels are common and may contribute to low energy levels.

d) Stay active as often as you can, for as long as you can. Especially important are leg, lower back and core strength activities that serve to increase balance, prevent falls, and facilitate mobility for longer periods. Keep pushing!

e) Keep the mind active. Even when bedridden, develop mental puzzles and games for the mind to 'chew on'. Keep the imagination alive - smile, laugh, love, create.

f) Don't allow today's symptoms to rob you of hope. Don't compare and contrast today to yesterday - and resist the urge to carry fear into tomorrow. Find reasons to celebrate each day, each moment, each success as they unfold.

g) More to come, of that I am certain!

March 15, 2013

My MSA Unawareness:

a) I forget that I can't run. I try to dodge raindrops. And busses.

b) I forget that I can't dance. Never could. But sometimes it looks like I'm trying. Actually, I'm just trying to get across the room.

c) I forget that I forget. When I get to the last page of a book, I think I may have already read that. Same with movies. And conversation. Wait . . .did I already say that?

d) I forget to say "no". I say yes to volunteering and lunch dates and all sorts of things that I'll likely have to cancel later.

e) I forget to say "yes". I say no when folks ask if I need help. No, I'm fine, I say - while lying here on the floor of my bathroom.

f) I forget to be a victim. I actually like forgetting.
Oh, sure, I have lots of reminders nagging at me, big and small, but I forget them.

So, that's my list. I'm sure I forgot something. That's cool with me.

April 2, 2013

W.A.D.E. through MSA, Part II:

W: water, water, water- consistent hydration day and night, is critical to neuro functioning.

A: accommodate to changing needs in mind, body and spirit- avoid comparing 'what is' to 'what was'.

D: vitamin D levels are key to maintaining immune systems and energy levels- take supplements, take sun.

38

E: eat less at any one time, but eat more often- avoid large, heavy meals, make healthy selections, and avoid eating late.

April 8, 2013

Ok, gang... have any of you experienced 'losing your mind'? It's hard to explain, and my doctors tell me it's from processing deficits, but it can be absolutely scary. It's as though a switch is thrown, and I struggle with sanity. I get horribly confused, disassociated, deeply depressed, and I can't come out from under it for a while.

The more I struggle to overcome this by trying to get my thoughts in order, the worse it gets. I suppose this experience may be defined as dementia - but I'd rather not admit that quite yet.... Luckily, I think today is going to be better!

April 26, 2013

Been taking stock of decisions I've made that seem to be helping...

- I cut out all artificial sweeteners and reduced sweets in general
- I greatly reduced my intake of fatty food, fried food and highly processed food
- I increased exercise when able to do so
- Alcohol disrupts sleep; marijuana assists with sleep seizures and reduces tremors.

May 3, 2013

Rotten night last night. Spasms, chills, numbness. I broke a rule: Limit sugars. I ate 2 doughnuts...and I knew better. Excess sugar causes me to have increased symptoms. You too?

May 13, 2013

This morning started out great - then, kinda tricked off into a long nap. Neuropathy has squatted in my forearms and hands and doesn't want to leave. I yell: "Out, out, damned neuropathy!"...but it does no good.

May 16, 2013

My diagnosis of MSA - Started off when my doctor noticed that my hands were shaking and thought it could be Benign Essential Tremor. But there was also ataxia present. I had ignored these symptoms for a while, as we often do. Blood work, labs, screenings. All negative.

Next, I was off to see a neurologist for assessment, including MRIs. Hmm, could it be cervical stenosis? Yes. Maybe. Time to consult with a neurosurgeon! Let's draw some spinal fluid and inject some dye and .... oh brother! Ouch! Nope, this isn't caused by stenosis. Let's try some physical therapy while we do more tests, more assessments. CAT scans, MRIs, clinical visits. Gonna send results to Mayo Clinic and Miami Jackson.

Meanwhile, I'm falling. A lot. This isn't fun - what's going on!? Confirmation of something from Mayo? Yes, yes, we think we have an answer. Hey, MSA? What the heck is MSA? Oh, gee, that's not good. And the journey- and the learning- began. I'm so grateful for a skilled team of Drs!

May 18, 2013

Planning life around MSA is a lot like trying to track a hurricane . . . while your busy gathering data, it's already changed course, speed and intensity. And ain't no plywood gonna help.

May 20, 2013

Used this weak day to compare the etymology of MSA with that of Chronic Traumatic Encephalopathy. I've grown more convinced that the origin of my neuro issues can be traced back to a series of head traumas - which were numerous and often serious. The correlation between MSA and head injury, while studied, has not been verified and remains an area to be further explored. Of course, in the end, neither MSA nor Chronic Traumatic Encephalopathy can be effectively treated - so maybe I should just relax and take another nap.

May 22, 2013

Had the strangest dream last night. I was back in the classroom, teaching 4th graders about leadership, when my voice started to give out. I waited awhile, then started over - and, again, my voice failed me. Then my legs wobbled and went out from under me. I fell to the floor in a heap. The kids came and tried to make me comfortable, using their sweaters and jackets to cushion my head and cover my body. Then, they went back to their assignments. I waited for help, but it never came.

Eventually, the dismissal bell rang, and the students left, saying "goodbye" on their way out the door. After some time, I managed to make my way down the hallway, passing new teachers whose faces I didn't know. They each nodded or waved as they went by. When I got to the parking lot, next to my car, I fell again. End of dream sequence. This is the first year in the past 25 that I am not involved in end-of-year school activities. Guess it nags at me a bit . . . Whatchya think, Freud?

THE JOURNEY IS MADE EASIER WITH FRIENDS.

dataMSA.com

June 26, 2013

Today's MSA Tip: MSA & Stress - it's a Heller "Catch 22" situation. Stress exacerbates MSA symptoms - but having MSA symptoms is stressful. Oh, what to do, what to do?

Try:

a) meditation/relaxation/deep breathing techniques

b)   moderate   exercise   when   possible

c)   avoiding   sugary   and   fatty   processed   junk   food

d)   no   caffeine   after   your   mid-morning   'kickstart'

e)   no   alcohol   (that's   a   tough   one!)

f)   getting   enough   interrupted   REM   sleep

g)   avoiding   taking   on   too   many   challenges

h)   adopting an AAA plan: assess, accept, adapt

June 30, 2013

Today's MSA Tip: Will Power (no, not that kind . . .).

It brings peace of mind to have all your legal affairs sorted as you transition through MSA. Do you have a designated health care surrogate (and, more importantly, has that person agreed to do so)? Who has Power of Attorney in case you are unable to manage large decisions? Do you wish to be an organ donor? Is your will drawn and up to date?

If you don't have resources to hire an attorney, documents can be uploaded online from a variety of 'estate planning' sites. Complete them, have witness(es) sign and make certain folks know where to find these documents in case of emergency. Your health surrogate and whoever has Power of Attorney should have copies for their files.

Now, you can rest easy. Take a nice deep breath. Or a nap. Or a deep breath and then a nap!

July 17, 2013

Well gang, despite yesterday's post about depression, I awoke at 5 this morning, crying. Tears filled my eyes. There is no panacea (at least I got to sleep!).

So, today's MSA Tip of the Day:

- Surrender All Hope for Better Yesterdays.

I find myself often wondering what might have been if MSA had not sneaked into my life. The lost opportunities, the lost potential. If I could go back to my 'healthy days', what would I do differently?

I often dream (as I did last night) of being back at work, or back to my hobbies, but knowing (even in sleep) that I can no longer perform the tasks. I think of who I 'used to be' and it takes me down a few notches.

But none of us gets a 'Mulligan', a do-over. And while, it's natural to have moments of 'self-pity', regret is an altogether different matter. Smile proudly and be grateful to have had the experiences you've had - and will continue to have - because there are many who were denied the privilege. Then, happily allow yourself to surrender all hope for better yesterdays!

July 18, 2013

'Morning, gang! Had a fine night's sleep –

Today's MSA Tip of the Day - for caregivers and others:
-- On those days when we MSA folk seem to be in a coma, when we can't get our eyes to open, or our legs to work. When we can't speak, and our breathing is labored. When we lie motionless for hours . . . we can hear you. We may not respond, but we can hear. In fact, my hearing is especially keen during those times. And our minds are still active. So, remember that we are there. Talk to us, but please don't talk about us . . . cuz we're gonna know!

July 2, 2013

Good morning! Here's Today's MSA Tip: Purrin' and Waggin'! Pets add so much to our lives and can be great companions for us MSA folks. My dog, Lady, and my cat, Crosley, stay by my side when I am bedridden - and make my day so much better! But sometimes pets can get underfoot, or tug at their leashes. For those of us with balance issues, extra care is needed! Boy oh boy, it's worth it for moments like this.

July 10, 2013

Good morning, fair lads and lasses! For the past 2 nights, I have slept like a log! But as we know - logs don't really sleep. I need some Zzzzs! Here's the MSA Tip of the Day: SSD/Medicare-What I have Learned - (get ready, it's long).Two years from the date of your SSD eligibility, you will be automatically enrolled in Medicare Part A and can enroll in Part B at a minimal cost. This is great news for those of us who face high health insurance premiums (even through COBRA). But - here's a little-known tidbit:

If you are under 65 and try to purchase Medicare Supplement Insurance, your premiums may be 2.5-3 times higher than those paid by folks 65 and older. Yes, 'tis true. Private carriers set the prices for their supplemental policies. One policy I reviewed would have cost nearly $800/mo. So, what are the options for those of us who aren't "Gotrocks"?

The Medicare Advantage plans (run by private carriers but overseen by Medicare) usually carry no premium over the Medicare Part B payment. However, they operate like an HMO--with a primary provider managing care- and your doctors may not be part of the system. Within Advantage plans, there are options, as well - sort of like a High Option HMO. You can learn more by locating your state's Medicare webpage. It will list the plans available - but not the prices. And you may want to contact your doctors to learn which plans, if any, they participate in. Yes, it pays to do homework! Now, here's another little-known nugget - when you are first eligible for Medicare A&B, you have a window of time to make your decisions. If you wait too long, you may not be eligible for the Advantage plans - for once the window of time closes, they do not have to accept you. And, for those in SSD, under age 65, they likely won't. And - note this:

If you are under 65, once you make a decision for either standard Medicare, Part B or an Advantage plan you CANNOT switch to the other until you are 65! Yep, it's true. You can switch providers during the open enrollment period in the fall, but you cannot go from Advantage to standard Part B or vice-versa. For me, the wait would be nearly 10 years! So, do your due diligence and decide carefully. Whew, time for a sweet-tea (decaffeinated) and a nap. My head hurts! But I hope your Hump day is fine as kind!

July 15, 2013

Beware the Ides of July? Nah. Today's MSA Tip of the Day: Value. Each of us likes to feel important in some way . . . to feel that we have value. It can be quite difficult for MSA folks to watch others get on with their days, their lives, while they are unable to keep up. Many of us have given up our careers, our social events, even some friendships, because of our limitations.

So, it's very important that we all find something to engage ourselves - no matter how small it may seem. As caregivers, reach

46

out. Ask for our thoughts, our opinions. Involve us - Try to keep us visible, viable and valuable!

July 16, 2013

Today's MSA Tip of the Day: Depression Awareness - something near, but not so dear, to me - Facing MSA in its many forms can surely be depressing, for both patients and caregivers. To make things worse, MSA can create chemical depression, as well. A 1-2 punch in the emotional gut. So, what to do? Obviously, there are the traditional answers - exercise, proper diet, hobbies. Ok, yes -well - they only go so far (and do precious little for chemical depression). Therapy? Counseling? Yes, often helpful for the caregiver(s) - but can the MSA patient get out for appointments regularly and as scheduled? And perhaps costs are a factor, even with insurance. Again, not to appear negative, but chemical depression responds poorly to counseling/therapy as the only intervention.

I must admit, it took me a long time to accept that psychotropic medication was a viable option. I hated the thought; I resisted the suggestions from my doctors. But, eventually, I relented, Now, I see it as a part of my treatment planning. Medication with therapy has helped me adjust to the many and continuing challenges.

July 19, 2013

Happy Friday, my friends! Today's End of the Week MSA Tip (more of a thought) of the Day: Mind, Body and Soul

I've kind of accepted that my brain is going a bit bonkers - but I don't equate my brain with my mind. My mind still holds great

47

capacity for creative thought, expression, compassion and so forth. In order to keep my mind healthy and active, I must work to align my spiritual self (my soul) to harmony and faith (in whatever form that may take) for I believe that faith and fear cannot coexist in my thoughts. And the body, whenever willing, is the vehicle for my will - so it too requires maintenance. I watch what I eat, I try to perform basic exercise whenever I am able. And I celebrate all three forms of my being - mind, body and soul. So, don't let a short in the wiring destroy your entire structure! Anyone know a good electrician? Happy Friday.

July 20, 2013

Today's MSA Tip of the Day is really warning, and a reminder - one I know we've all heard before. But it bears repeating this summer: Beware of heat exhaustion! It's a great danger to us MSA folk.

Yesterday, I went to lunch with friends to an outside, waterfront restaurant. We had to walk a fair distance to the car. And it's July. And it's hot. Bad decision. When I got home, I fell into bed for 90 minutes - out like a stone.

By then it was time to walk Lady the Wonder Dog. After her rounds, I hadn't noticed I wasn't perspiring - at all, despite the 90' heat. I put the dog in the house and brought the trash can to the curb for pick up. Suddenly, it hit. I started to go down. I made it to the front door, but somehow, I had locked myself out. I didn't have the strength to reach the backdoor. I knew I was in trouble - but I blacked out.

At some point, a kind neighbor found me, helped me inside and called 911. After all the usual assessments, paramedics found that I was not dehydrated and that my blood pressure, blood sugar, etc. was ok - however, they suggested that I go to the hospital. I declined. Might have been a foolish mistake, but after getting into the a/c and some cold compresses, I made it all right - although it was a rough night. Today, I was weak as water - but am now coming around.

Some of you are keenly aware of this issue. I thought I was, too - but I made some critical, dangerous mistakes. So, my friends, MSA or not, be very careful. This heat can be devastating! From now on, I'll be chillin'

July 30, 2013

Good morning, my friends! Today's MSA Tip of the Day: Losing Touch! (literally, this time)

I find I drop things easily because I can't always 'feel' them in my hands. To increase my sense of touch, I gently GENTLY rub my fingertips and thumb (does that count as a finger?) with a pumice stone once a week. You can find these stones at any drug store in the 'foot care' aisle. It does help me - but it doesn't make it any easier to eat soup with a spoon! Have a good day - I hope to.

July 31, 2013

Good morning, gang! Hope you are doing OK! It occurred to me last night (when I couldn't get to sleep, again) that it was only 3 years ago this summer I was diagnosed.

Ahhh, yes - the Summer of 2010! It brought us such hits as "I Wanna Hold Your Hand (but why does it shake so much?)" , "Free Fallin" (Tom Petty) , "Starin' at the Ceiling" (Keane) & "Head

Over Heels" (Tears for Fears). Everyone was talking about 'Spinal Tap', but I was keeping an eye on 'The New Scans'. My favorite 'one hit wonder' was: "I've Fallin and I Can't Get Up and I Hit My Head So Hard I Had a Seizure!" Great tune.

Business news for the Summer of 2010 included: "Forced Job Resignation" and "25-Year Career Brought to a Screeching Halt" Real estate headlines stated, "Why You Have to Move - Because, Silly, You Can No Longer Afford to Live Here."

The Food & Health Sections also had feature stories that summer: "Foods That Might Choke You Up" , "The Heimlich- It's Not Just for Strangers Anymore", and "Damaged Brain Cells: We're Here, We're Weird, Get Used to It." Of course, top billing went to "Clinical Trials: They're Not for Everyone and they get your hopes up and when they fail you are devastated for a really long time." Good reading there.

Ahh, yes. What a summer. Seems like only yesterday . . . But this is the summer of '13 - let's make it the best! "I Know You Want It"!

August 1, 2013

. . . to modify a quote by Winston Churchill: "I cannot forecast to you the action of (MSA) - it is a riddle wrapped in a mystery inside an enigma."

August 3, 2013

A little too dark. A little too stormy.
Yesterday found me incapacitated and bed-bound for hours and hours on end. Mutiny, I tell you . . . full-on mutiny. It felt like I was

trudging through a deep swamp in teaming rain and making no progress whatsoever.

But then came night - and the storm worsened. My mind went berserk and began to present a variety of MSA doomsday scenarios, each one poking mercilessly at my soul.

Finally, I surrendered all hope of sleep. I turned on reruns of something mindless to keep my mad mind distracted. Hour upon hour . . . a torturous combination of short-circuited thinking and idiotic TV commercials.

Then, at dawn, the sun rose. The room brightened. My eyes came into new focus. And here I am, ready to go at the world again. Like a south Florida hurricane, there is calm and beauty after the storm passes.

I FOCUS ON THE BATTLE OF EACH DAY AS MY STRATEGY IN THE WAR AGAINST MSA.

I PUSH. I PUSH HARD.

DO WHATEVER YOU CAN, WHENEVER YOU CAN, THEN DO A BIT MORE.

August 6, 2013

Good morning, children - I hope today brings you "all things wise and wonderful!" Today's MSA Tip of the Day is really a warning: Ambien!

I keep a vial of Ambien at the ready for those desperate nights when sleep is elusive. With one little 'helper', I get a good night's rest. But "danger, danger, Will Robinson!"

Last night, in an Ambien trance, I fell out of bed, crashed into a dresser and landed on the floor. Dean got me back into bed. The best part is - I remember NONE of it!

Today, I feel as if I lost a fight. My arm has some sort of damage (that I'm certain will heal up quickly). For now, I think I'll leave those pills in their little bottle - which, in turn, will leave me in the safety of my little bed! Zzzzzzz

August 21, 2013

. . . although MSA shuts me down when it chooses, I am grateful to still be able to pursue meaning in my life. I find fulfillment in my hobbies and my interests - but mostly in volunteering when I can. It keeps me going - I receive much more than I can ever give.

August 27, 2013

Ok, lads and lasses - here is the latest from my world of neurology: YIPPEEE! Yes, that's right - YIPPEE! Now, I have never said YIPPEE after a neuro visit before but, today truly caused a YIPPEE reaction . . . and here's why: It appears this MSA 'companion' I have been living with may have become a bit less aggressive - and could actually be slowing down. Yes . . . YIPPEE! But why? What is the cause?

I discussed the possibilities with my neurologist. One, I have seriously altered my diet; Two, I have stayed as socially active as possible through volunteer work, etc.; Three, I try with all my heart to stay positive and determined.

He shared details from Alzheimer's-related studies that indicate these 3 issues can affect outcomes - especially maintaining or increasing social interactions. He stated that it is essential to have face-to-face interactions often and with a variety of folks in a variety of settings (if possible). I have truly tried to do that when I can.

Less certain is the effect of diet, although there are a number of studies linking dietary intake with neuro functioning. I cut or greatly reduced artificial sweeteners, additives, and so forth. I avoid all processed foods and limit sugar and fat to small amounts.

And I try to be as active as I can when I can. On my 'lost days', when I am bedridden, I keep my mind going by planning or problem solving. When I am able to get up, I go! I try to keep my body going - although, in summer's heat, it can be tricky.
So, that's the YIPPEE news. Not cures, not all better - but hopeful, as always. And extremely grateful.

August 28, 2013

Well, I guess I got a bit overexcited yesterday because today found me a little off. Legs wonky, eyes goofy, and very worn out. But heck - I have it better than many on the globe. Regarding yesterday's neuro update, there are 2 other variables:

Stress- I do all I can to lessen areas of stress because it leaves me a trembling, incoherent being. After years of handling a rather stressful job, I now find my 'systems' responding poorly to any gravel or bumps in the road. So, I try to plan ahead and prepare whenever possible. Proactive problem-solving!

Cannabis- I know this is a controversial area, and there are countless studies regarding cannabis and neurological responses. I can only speak from my experiences. I was somewhat of a nerd in the 70s, 80s, 90s (well, you get the idea) and I never used cannabis. However, for the past 1.5 years or so, I ingest cannabis about 2 hours before bedtime. It helps with uninterrupted sleep (otherwise, I get 90 minutes at a clip) - it helps with digestive discomfort, and it relieves eye fatigue and pain.

Now, could consistent use of cannabis be helping in other ways? I can't say but, I do believe it helps with these symptoms.

At any rate, I hope you are doing well today - this very historic day. Cheers!

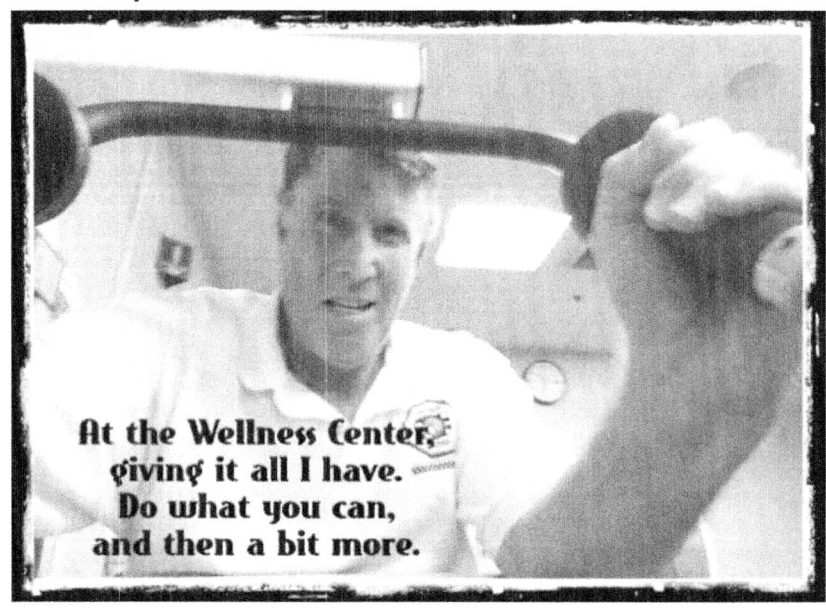

At the Wellness Center,
giving it all I have.
Do what you can,
and then a bit more.

It can be quite hard to face that we may be losing our battle against MSA. But we must understand that there are personal battles for each of us in this life - and no matter how worn we may become, we must never surrender.

For what we may lose in mind and body, we gain in Spirit - and it is our Spirit that will triumph on this plane and those that follow.

This is me at age 19. I was a bit wild~

August 31, 2013

Thought of the Day - this hot, steamy summer day - I have been fortunate to have enjoyed very good health for much of my life - and I knew it. In HS, I volunteered to help children with cerebral palsy and muscular dystrophy (met Jerry Lewis!). I learned to appreciate my life that much more. In college, I worked with suicide prevention and did fundraising for folks in need. Later, I focused on pediatric AIDS and homeless youth.

I guess what I am trying to say is, you don't have to wait for illness or bad circumstances to affect you or your family directly before getting involved. Of course, I want there to be a cure for MSA. I want there to be a focus on research and development.

But you may have your own projects which you feel strongly about - and I surely respect that!

So, make a promise to be proactive. Find a need in the community and go about making it better. Get involved for the purest reason - it is a good and right thing to do. Because, what affects one of us, eventually affects each of us. Now, go at 'em!

September 3, 2013

Yesterday's passage was truly challenging . . .worse than the day before. All systems went 'off-line'...except, oddly, hearing- which remained sharp and keen. No sleep at all last night. Although this morning finds me greatly compromised,

I know that the seas will calm-

The wind will change direction-

The sun will shine.

September 8, 2013

- Slower than a feeding mullet.
- Less powerful than his emotions.
- Able to leave small buildings with a single cane.
- Look! Up at this guy!
- Not preferred! Can't explain!
- It's Stupor, man!

Yes, Stupor, man, with strange feelings from another dimension. With no powers and abilities at all like those of normal men. Stupor, man, who, disguised as mild-mannered me, living in a somewhat great metropolitan area, Fights his daily battle for truth, justice. And ways to cope with MSA!

September 9, 2013

Good grief! Yesterday, I could barely keep my eyes open. Slept and slept and slept hour after hour. The entire day long. So, today, I expect to have super-extraordinary energy, Like Superman. Stay tuned!

September 11, 2013

Update: Legs formed a union and went on strike today. I'd say it was a 'walk-out', but that would be too ironic. They were demanding early retirement. Of course, I said, 'no way'. They wouldn't budge. Neither would I. Or, rather, neither could I.

At any rate, we began negotiations while I lay in bed. I offered to support their efforts through canes and walkers and so forth yet, I found them to be rather unfeeling -despite my protestations, they sat numbly. I think we may have reached agreement, however. They have agreed to work part-time. On and off. Now and again. All I ask is that they don't quit.

September 24, 2013

Been a rough day. I feel old for my 56 years. Some days, I struggle with my 'new' brain. It's more impulsive, more sensitive to stress. Its functioning is familiar and yet quite different. It's at once intriguing . . .and frightening. Tomorrow, I expect to feel like a young man again. Thank goodness for tomorrow...

September 25, 2013

...some days, I feel that the weakness and fatigue will overtake me. I just want to lay in bed, close my eyes and pray for total healing for me and many others. but that's not good enough.

I still have the energy to push back - to not allow the voice of rambling fears in my mind to grow to a roar. so, today - this day - I celebrate what and where I am. I express gratitude for my life and strive to improve situations for those less lucky than I.

September 26, 2013

Oh, good grief. I seldom get 'down' with this MSA rot but, today I wanted to shed a tear or two. It's the sheer frustration of not being able to do the things I could easily do only a short time ago. It seems everything is slowly failing me, and I keep trying to adjust, bit by bit . . . whew.

Ok, enough self-pity. Onward.

September 27, 2013

Good morning, gang! Sorry for my wallowing in pity yesterday. Sometimes, the still of a sleepless night becomes the perfect setting for reflection. Dean and I had a good long talk about the reality of our situation - which I usually avoid trying to protect him. Then, I sat up for a few hours with my own thoughts.

I want to waste no more time worrying about the future, the past, friends lost, insensitive statements and other rot. I hope to realize, in each moment, my thanks for being alive, for having whatever abilities present that day. I know how to do this - I lost track.

Most importantly, I must realign myself within the stream of energy's consciousness. When we stray too far from this alignment, we experience more 'dis-ease'. We mustn't allow ourselves to become trapped by flotsam and jetties, whirlpools and jams, while Life's energy flows on.

So today, this day, I will better prepare myself. I will focus. That is, if I can get both eyes to stay open at once.

September 30, 2013

Ok, kids - do any of you experience any of the following - you can answer by letter (I know, this sounds like an ad for some new pharmaceutical):

If you have ALWAYS had these, like me, just indicate if they have worsened.
I'm just so curious about MSA and cognition...

a) immediate short-term memory loss (like, um… wait... what was I asking?)

b) confused or muddled thinking

c) brain 'freezes' (not from ice cream) where your thoughts jam up and stop

d) perseveration - fixating on thoughts or plans . . . over and over and over

e) lower frustration levels, shorter temper, quicker to anger

f) increased impulsivity

g) processing, problem-solving and decision-making deficits.

October 4, 2013

Yesterday was bittersweet.

- So, moving to see the tributes to the many worldwide lost to MSA - brought tears to my eyes —

- So good to know there are many kind folks out there rallying for all of us - for awareness, for treatment, for support –
- And yet, so frightening to know what may lie ahead in my path.

But today I smile. As long as there is sweet air in my lungs and life's blood rushing in my veins- there will be joy and appreciation in my heart.

October 6, 2013

Happy Sunday, my friends! Yesterday was 'lost'. That's what I call the days in which I either sleep for many hours on end or can do nothing for myself - or both.

But, by mid-evening, I had rallied! I was able to get up, run a comb through my hair, have something to eat, watch TV - I was almost a 'real boy' again.

This morning, I feel much better. I hear the birds chirping and the neighborhood coming to life. I'm not sure what I will do with today, but my goal is to make the best of it! I think I can, I think I can - I know I can!

October 18, 2013

-interesting discussion regarding the difficulty receiving an MSA diagnosis - As an 'abstract' thinker . . .I would prefer to receive a misdiagnosis, with some level of hope - rather than a 'correct' diagnosis, but without any hope for treatment or cure.

In fact, I often convince myself that I don't have MSA at all - that there is some other malady causing my symptoms.

Just a mind game - You may say I'm a dreamer - but I'm not the only one . . .

October 19, 2013

Morning, all! Happy Friday. Had a rough go the past two days - exhausted. Interesting, though, how fast I lose track of time and days...

"Where are you going, my Tuesday, like yesterday,

Where are you going, my Wednesday, my time?

Turn around and it's two,

Turn around and it's four,

Turn around and time slips by, just past my door.

Turn around, turn around,

Turn around and life slips by, just past my door."

October 31, 2013

- Beware all things that go bump in the night! Our story begins weeks ago, when it was I who went bump in the night. I fell from bed and had a collision with a large dresser. Banged up my elbow and knee - and the right side of my face - a bit. The following day, I felt like a jack-o-lantern in summer - rotten. But, as usual, I got on with things.

Several days later, a small area under my cheekbone kept bothering me, as did my jaw. I chalked it up to the fall. When it didn't get better, I thought it was because I might be clenching my teeth at night. Or the way I have to position myself in bed to be able to breath. There was no pain when I brushed or flossed - but it was getting harder and harder to open my mouth.

Those of us living with MSA face the continual challenge of adapting to or coping with new and ever-changing situations. I am rather used to it - but this was different. Something serious was going on, and it was hiding under MSA-like issues.

This Monday, my face puffed up like a pumpkin and my upper right gum looked like a horror scene. I got in to see my dentist right away and after x-rays and examinations, he couldn't be sure of the cause. Off to the oral surgeon.

To condense this harrowing story, apparently that fall not only jarred my jaw and mouth, it likely created an infection (who's symptoms I credited to other situations). This infection spread throughout the right side of my face, settled into my sinuses, my ear canal, around 3 teeth and into the hinge of my jaw. In the time it had to fester, it caused bone loss in teeth, my jaw and my jaw hinge. I lost one tooth as a result (damn!). My trick-or-treat goody bag this year is filled with antibiotics, pain killers, medical rinses, gauze and future office visit cards!

The moral of the story: Any kind of infection can be bad news for folks with MSA - Don't ignore pain, swelling or other persistent symptoms.

Now, go out there and have a good time! BOO!

November 8, 2013

Thirty-five years ago, this month, my father lost his footing and ended his life.

It took me many years to cope, to adjust, to understand.

From his actions that day, I learned to make something from what I was given. And this damned MSA will never take that away from me.

November 12, 2013

Back to see my new friend, Mr. Oral Surgeon, tomorrow morning . . . geesh, his darned antibiotics had the same reaction I experienced during the Rifampicin trials - they nearly did me in!

Got to the point I could barely eat because of the discomfort that will appear a bit later. Lesson learned - don't ignore pains and swelling after a bad fall!

November 28, 2013

Come on, gang - sing along!
"From the Day of Diagnosis, MSA gave to me -

Twelve months in a study
Eleven Rifampicin refills
Ten trips and tumbles
Nine neuro-assessments
Eight insurance hassles
Seven treatment searches
Six acupuncture sessions
Five "Woe - is - Me's"
Four trips to Mayo
Three ambulance rides
Two spinal taps
And a hope for us to be healed!

December 2, 2013

Off to see Dr. Neuro first thing tomorrow - here's what I have to discuss:
- Been choking a bit more on a bit less. The antibiotic for my oral surgery, Augmentin has nearly killed me to death. I often get heated or chilled - like brie and white wine.

But, overall, I am one happy camper! Many days, I can still get out - some days I can walk the shoreline. I volunteer about 1 day a week and every now and again, I can play with my little British cars or my old boat.

I have great friends, a loyal dog and a loving partner.

What more could I ask for? Lucky me!

December 3, 2013

Well, gang - I got a darned good report after today's neuro-assessment.

The after-effects of the Augmentin are tapering off and, given the dosage I was on, were not at all unusual. However, if I must face something similar, I know to seek pre-treatment to lessen the discomfort. MSA and strong antibiotics can be a very bad mix.

My gate has not worsened and, in fact, may have improved. This may be due to my beach walks (when I am able). My legs are stronger and my balance better.

To reduce choking episodes, I must be more cautious about what I eat - and NO CARBONATED DRINKS (even Guinness?)

There is little to be done about the chills that overcome me, except to avoid exposure to heat (should be easier this time of year!). Response to excessive heat can come hours after exposure.

But, perhaps the most exciting news is that it appears that the progression has slowed a great deal in the past 6 months! I'm to meet with Dr again a bit later to conduct further assessments and to discuss the strategies I use that could be contributing to success.

I do believe that diet, exercise, meditation and socialization have helped a good bit. Ingesting cannabis each night allows for restful (and REM) sleep - and who knows what else?!

And Dean is always there with love and support - and that brings me great comfort and peace. More later – Cheers, mates!

December 4, 2013

I was awkwardly reminded today that there is frustration bubbling within me,

- hidden by a smile,

- underneath the optimism,

- in the shadow of hope.

I sometimes feel like standing on a rooftop and screaming, "You guys just don't understand!" But, of course, they can't - because I don't. So, I smile at the folly, draw a deep breath and take a nap.

December 11, 2013

Had a visit with my general practitioner today - the fall I took a while back caused some damage to my face (which I already knew-lost a tooth!).

What I didn't know was how badly I hurt my jaw. Gonna take some more time for that heal up.

And the 1750 mg of amoxicillin daily wiped out my poor digestive system (many of us MSA folk already face those challenges!). However, time should heal that up a bit. But all in all, I am quite healthy - good BP, healthy heart rate…

December 15, 2013

Yesterday may have been my worst yet, could barely move at all, hour upon hour - my flame was dim, but the embers were still burning within.

December 20, 2013

This Christmas I'd like for you, my friends, to wish that I be cured of MSA - but I can't. Because I'd like for you to wish that all those who suffer, all those with illness will be healed, will be cured. Because MSA doesn't make me special or different. I'm no more deserving of healing than those who stand beside me.

So, this year as we wish and hope and pray, let's resolve to also take action -to be there for each other, to uplift one another.

And that, my friends, is truly a gift where 'one size fits all'.

MY
PERSPECTIVE
HAS BEEN
FOREVER
ALTERED.

68

2014

January 9, 2014

...it's rainy and dank here in South Florida but, no complaints! Despite some emotional setbacks, I continue to pursue the voices of individuals living with MSA. I feel there is a distinct need for current patients to have a platform where they may share experiences, fears, goals and hopes -free from the influences and observations of others. I have become keenly aware that the majority of the members living with MSA seek more privacy.

February 9, 2014

I'm jetsam, drifting on a raft into waters of which I know little - where the horizon is blurred and boundaries between day and night seem nonexistent.

I can't be certain if my thoughts are that of dreams or reality because my mind seems set on playing tricks -mean spirited tricks.

Currents and tides pull me along and I have no way to overcome them. Perhaps, they know best

February 10, 2014

Had to go to court today regarding property I own. I tremored so much I couldn't button my shirt. Glad it's over . . . for now. Stress reduces me to Jell-O.

February 25, 2014

wicked day-

weak, worn,

wondering why.

why this day?

systems in mutiny,

hour upon hour.

nothing cooperating

nothing communicating.

but,

it will all pass in time . . .

the sun also rises-

March 6, 2014

As Week 1 of MSA Awareness Month draws to a close –

I am thankful for my friends, near and far, who share their lives with me.

I am thankful for the friends who check in on me, who help me on my challenging days, who keep my spirits lifted.

I am thankful for the friends who share their day with me, who get me out and about, who give me new things to think about.

I am thankful for the friends who help me remember that MSA does not define me. Thanks, everyone!

March 7, 2014

My MSA cycle was pretty darned good this week, until today. . .when I find myself as limp as a dish rag.

That's ok. I take the good with the not so good, as we all do...

70

March 8, 2014

My legs feel like wood,

my head, like putty-

and I have the strength

of wet crepe paper.

I'm some sort of

wacky craft project . . .

but, I am thankful for each day!

March 16, 2014

Today, I've decided. I'm tired of MSA. I mean, I've tried to
be a good sport,

taking it all in stride,

staying stoic,

head into the wind,

etc. etc. yada yada –

But, today, I've had enough. Of course, there's not a damned
thing I can do about it that I haven't already done a thousand
times or more.

So, I'm pissed.

There. I said it.

Now, I'll get on with the day.

March 20, 2014

Happy First Day of Spring - a season of new possibilities!

Today, Day 20 of MSA Awareness Day,
I am thankful for my own possibilities –

In July 2010, I began my diagnostic process and was given a prognosis of 66-72 months. In October 2012, after finishing a clinical trial, I received a prognosis of 30-36 months.

But (+) results from recent neuro assessments indicate that those numbers are no longer valid - not that they really ever were . . .

March 24, 2014

Gee, this month is passing me by quickly!
Day 24 of MSA Awareness Month and today, I am expressing gratitude for all the folks who have participated in the data*MSA Survey for Multiple System Atrophy.

This morning, I sent our most recent data report to the Neuro Department @ Mayo Clinic, JAX. But it seems some surveys haven't come through yet -and the more data, the better!

So, please invite all others in our wide-spread, very diverse MSA Community to participate in this patient-driven survey. Thanks, always – BILL

May 27, 2014

. . . here's hoping that a challenging night leads to a carefree day. Hey, sometimes hope is all we have!

March 28, 2014

TGIF(s): Thank Goodness I Finally Slept! I hope you have your own TGIF, whatever that may look like!

March 30, 2014

I wasn't able to post yesterday - so, I'll express thanks this morning. I am thankful to be here.

In my early 30's, I nearly succumbed to emotional pain from childhood abuse, planning to end my life as my father had years before.

But, in the weakest of moments a spiritual voice lifted me and caused me to seek help - so I could see things differently so I could focus on strength rather than weakness -light, rather than darkness.

And today I am very grateful to be able to speak of it.

April 2, 2014

Something went very wrong today . . . I suddenly lost a large section of my memory. I am hopeful it's temporary . . . it's very unsettling.

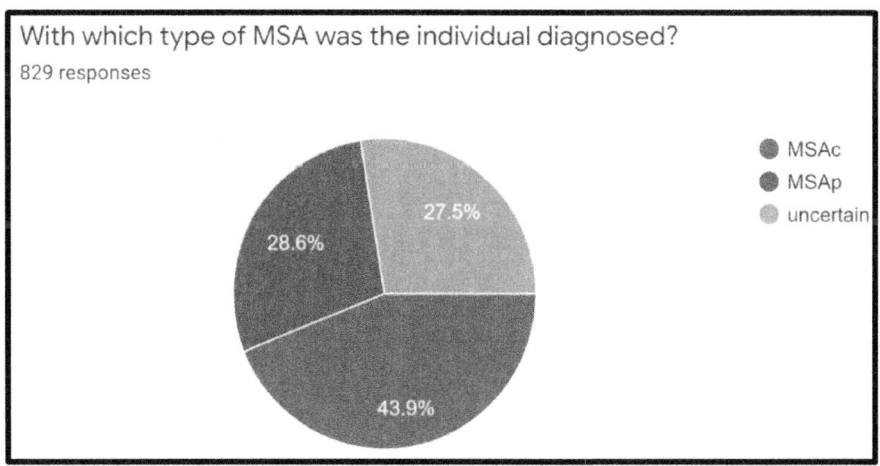

April 11, 2014

After a restless night -I came to an understanding. What frightens me most about facing MSA - what causes me to shudder, to tense, to scream inside - stems from an unbridled anger that one day I will find myself totally dependent at the hand of others. I've spent a lifetime avoiding that situation with an almost pathological fervor.

Acceptance won't come easily. Nor quietly.

April 21, 2014

Here in these wee hours, dark dreams have kidnapped my sleep as they have done many nights.

The restraints I use against fearful thoughts loosen as my mind drifts and seeks its own path.

Tonight, I

Some days, you just seek comfort.

dataMSA.com

awoke quickly -my pulse racing, my breathing quick and shallow.

It's better when I come 'round this way. I avoid wrestling with unconquerable threats that loom in the shadows of reality.

74

The salvation of daylight advances with the slow but steady hands of the clock and all will be bright and beautiful again.

April 28, 2014

Anyone who might like to better understand how stress affects neuro-functioning should spend some time with me today. After 3+ years of stable care, my world is rocked.   I   am   so overwhelmed by insurance, doctors, specialists and referrals that I can barely keep my eyes open and focused.

I'm not sure I can navigate all of this without help. I'm   so   weary,   but   sleep   isn't   always   a   respite. Depression is wafting in . . .

May 5, 2014

Today was a 'mixed-bag' –

(+) I did manage to get an appointment set up with my neurologist, after being told I could no longer see him. (-) I haven't a lick of energy left after dealing with all of this insurance flim-flam.

(+) Despite the obstacles, I get to stay with my doctor... and that will allow me to sleep easier.

(-) I was nearly too worn down to remain (+)!

May 22, 2014

. . . isn't life interesting? In the middle of my rather dismal, but typical MSA Thursday, I received a note from the Program Director of the National Institute of Neurological Disorders and Stroke (NINDS)/National Institutes of Health (NIH).

NINDS is quite interested in the data*MSA Survey for Multiple System Atrophy and invited data*MSA to be a part of the Autonomic Disorders Consortium (ADC) under the Rare Diseases Clinical Research Network (RDCRN).

This is, indeed, quite good news and will allow for the expansion of survey participants and longitudinal study for individuals affected by MSA, both living and lost.

I will let you know as things progress - and, while I remained stuck in bed - this did put a smile on my face!

May 24, 2014

. . . are my weak days coming closer together or, am I pushing myself a bit too hard lately?

May 31, 2014

In spite of my continued optimism -some things are changing: - increased irregularity of sleep cycles. . . (yes, it's 4am here)

- worsening swallowing issues

- aspirating saliva

- increased eye fatigue, sensitivity

- worsening fine motor skills

But overall - I am one lucky man! I'm beating my prognosis - and that's a fine thing!

June 4, 2014

What a fine day! Raining here, but I like that. Had lunch with some good, good friends from my days in education - so bright they are . . . so many ideas!

As usual, my steam runs out quickly. I can't accomplish nearly what I hope to –

As Scarlett said, "After all, tomorrow is another day." But, today - I need a nap.

June 5, 2014

These days - I anger quickly. Some of it is due to MSA rot. Some of it is due to facing the limits of time and that there is too little of it to waste.

So, if I seem to respond with anger -if my fuse seems short and my temper quick, it's because I have passion for what I believe in . . .and my ability to reign myself in is a bit impaired.

But it's mostly because our time here isn't infinite and there's so much to do . . .

Each day, by mid-morning, the tide of energy goes out and leaves me stranded...

June 11, 2014

When sleep slips from my grasp -I think.

a) How many persons (and their families) affected by MSA are living in or near poverty? How many were the primary or co -providers for their families and can no longer generate necessary income? What range of financial struggles has MSA created? How are these persons coping? Which of their needs may be going unmet?

b) Are persons of color less affected by MSA or do they not seek diagnosis due to a variety of factors? Is more awareness needed in communities of color and racial diversity?

I will try to address these topics (and others) in the data*MSA Survey 2.0! Hope you are well . . . I am rather exhausted, but far from defeated.

June 13, 2014

It was a lost day – or perhaps a day of healing. Simple, basic living tasks had to wait for help

-bathing alone is dangerous,

-eating alone leads to choking,

- getting to the toilet causes falls.

But each moment moves me closer to a new horizon . . .

June 23, 2014

In my profession, I employed a model out of Brown University in which one of the guiding principles was "Less = More". Let's see how this concept can be related to individuals affected by MSA:

- less agility = more falls

- less sleep = more exhaustion

- less ability = more frustration

Hmm . . . I think we can see how this concept can be applied, although it isn't quite the application the model intended! Now, let's try to apply the mathematical concept of "Equivalence Relation" . . . in this case, If "Less = More", then "More=Less":

- more progression = less ability

(or, in another light)

- more research = less 'guessing'

- more effective treatment = less suffering

- more voices = less silence

I've taken some liberties with logic here, but I prefer to label them as 'artistic license'. Other guiding principles of this model included,

- "Commitment to All" and

- "Democracy and Equity".

Interesting model . . .Interesting philosophy!

(it's 2:30 a.m. - less sleep = more random thinking!)

June 29, 2014

'changes in latitudes, changes in attitudes, nothing remains quite the same'. I hope this day brings you respite.

July 7, 2014

These days, my vision is growing weaker. Luckily, my imagination creates beauty in my mind's eye . . .

July 9, 2014

Got no deeds to do, no promises to keep. I'm dappled and drowsy and ready to sleep. Let the morning time drop all its petals on me. Life, I love you -doot-in' do-do-, all is groovy.

Yesterday was a lost day

from dawn to dusk

and dusk to dawn

hour upon hour

contained in my bed

as the world spun on it axis

but now the light of morning

is reaching out to include me

in a new and hopeful day.

dataMSA.com

I'm pretty darned useless today....

July 27, 2014

MSA be damned, I walked today. Wasn't at all easy, but I did it.

August 3, 2014

For the past few days, a strong tide lifted me and I nearly lost sight of my MSA rot.

Then, slowly, steadily. . .the water receded and symptoms reappeared like barnacles on old pilings.

But I know, that like the sun, the tide also rises . . . and I'll be waiting.

My MSA face...

This time of year, is rather bittersweet –

For an educator, there is a rhythm to the academic year. And, as for the kids, the end of the summer brings anticipation - (and if one is to be honest, a bit of dread).

I usually worked most of the summer. My special needs students required an extended school year - and I required the extra income. As the years progressed, I continued to work summers to feed my addiction to old cars and boats. And I enjoyed it. Summer sessions were more relaxed - I could implement more creative strategies.

Eventually, discussions among my colleagues became, "how long?" - meaning "how many years until retirement?" We each had our individual goals within our sites.

And then, MSA made its presence known to me. My career quickly shifted on the career ladder to stepping down into part-time hours. Then, into a series of personal and sick leaves. And, finally, a quiet resignation.

There would be no retirement parties. No 'count down calendars'. No jokes and hopes and dreams. Just an abrupt and unceremonious end to a two and half decade career.

All the stages of grief marched past and I nodded to each in my own time. Acceptance, though, hung back a bit and niggled at me. It still does.

And so, as a new school year sneaks up on us and kids squeeze the last bit of joy from summer before they occupy desks barely cold from June, I have signed on to volunteer at the school I attended as a boy. The staff there knows me - and my limitations - and I will be welcomed.

83

And I can happily regain the comforting rhythm I've been missing.

April 11, 2014

After a restless night -I came to an understanding. What frightens me most about facing MSA -what causes me to shudder, to tense, to scream inside - stems from an unbridled anger that one day I will find myself totally dependent at the hand of others .I've spent a lifetime avoiding that situation with an almost pathological fervor.

Acceptance won't come easily. Nor quietly.

August 13, 2014

I always try to be forthright on this page so I can provide an honest glimpse into my experiences living with MSA –

The recent discussion in the media about depression and its devastating effects is an important one . . . I have suffered with depression for nearly all of my adult life. At times, it was dire - and very frightening. I almost succumbed. When I finally sought treatment, I came to understand what life on the 'other side' looks like.

MSA can cause or exacerbate depression. I take an effective medication and, as of a month or so ago, have re-entered therapy 2x/month (I would go more often but finances restrict that).

Today, in session, my therapist suggested I delve back into my artwork, which I surrendered due to tremors. She senses a need, a vent for emotional expression. So, that's the plan. I rather expect the work to resemble chicken scratch, but it will be my chicken scratch - and no one has to see it.

And remember - you must take good care of yourself. Treat yourself well and seek help quickly if and when you need it. No need to suffer in silence - help is out there, close by. Trust me on this –

August 18, 2014

Thanks to my friends who inquired about my life with MSA! I'm 57. I was diagnosed with Multiple System Atrophy 4 years after a full year of extensive and often uncomfortable testing and assessments. I saw many neurologists, participated in a year-long clinical trial for an experimental drug and tried my damnedest to combat the outcomes.

My prognosis at the time of diagnosis was 55 - 60 months but I'm one of the fortunate; the progression of my illness has slowed a bit in the past 2 years. Generally, an individual survives 8- 10 years.

MSA is very rare, less than 200,000 people in the US population. I have MSA-P, which affects my involuntary (autonomic) functions: blood pressure, heart rate, bladder function, digestion, respiration, perspiration, sleep - as well as both my fine and gross motor skills. I have fallen many, many times, sometimes with very bad consequences. I've been hospitalized quite a few times. MSA also impacts my emotions, memory and cognition. I can get lost in the town I grew up in . . .

My MSA symptoms are irregular - on average, 1-2 days out of every 7, MSA severely impacts my ability to care for myself (from bathing, eating, toileting). At these times, speech, breathing and swallowing can be very difficult. I choke often. I struggle to breath. On my 'lost days', I cannot walk, and my limbs are nearly paralyzed.

Because of MSA, I had to surrender my teaching career and most of my savings, I was declared disabled and can no longer enjoy many of my hobbies and interests. It may seem to be hard on me - but I think it's much harder on Dean.

There's no known cause of Multiple System Atrophy (MSA) and there's no cure. Dean and I recognize the onset of worsening symptoms; when I am not well, I try to stay safe and comfortable to carry on.

The MSA Coalition sponsors fundraising for research and education - please visit their site and others like it.

I created a webpage from MSA patient-driven data I collected - it might help illustrate what the illness looks like to the individuals and their families: Thanks, again, for

asking me about MSA – BILL

August 20, 2014

To all the folks who have dedicated themselves to research and education of rare diseases throughout their lives...

- To the doctors, who commit themselves to a lifetime of work

- To the volunteers, who give of themselves hour upon hour, year upon year

- To the patients, who often go through agonizing experimental treatments for the benefit of others

- To the donors, who give generously to get research off the ground and keep it going

- To the loved-ones, who share painful experiences so that others can learn

- To all of you who remain "invisible", quietly working in the background; no YouTube videos, no Facebook posts, no name dropping.

I don't want to douse you with ice-water. No, no . . .I just want to say 'Thanks'! From the bottom heart - thanks for all you have done, for all you do, and will continue to do. You're my unsung heroes!

August 21, 2014

Morning, friends! ~ After a good night's sleep, I've come to realize I'm much like an old Jag V12 I used to own –

- hard to start

- hard to keep running

- prone to overheating

- problems in the wiring

- not worth what it once was

- and folks often say, "Well, it all looks fine to me!"

I hope it's 'Happy Motoring' throughout your day!

August 25, 2014

- each 1 reach 1 - This day, be an ambassador of help, hope and healing! This day, reach out to someone in need –

- someone suffering from debilitating illness

- someone who has exhausted their resources, both financially and emotionally

- someone whose family is weary from despair

This day, you can make a difference with simple acts of kindness and compassion.

This day, encourage others to join in because –

This day is the day that counts!

August 27, 2014

had therapy this morning - got to 'talk out' some of my feelings . . .my sympathies go out to my therapist! Remember, gang - share the challenge- "Each 1 Reach 1" Lend a hand to someone suffering from debilitating neurological disease. (ALS, Alzheimer's, MS, MSA, Parkinson's, etc.)

They need you.

August 29, 2014

Did you know that, in the US - (approx.)?

- 15,000-20,000 people suffer with MSA

- 30,000 people suffer with ALS

- 400,000 people suffer with Multiple Sclerosis

- 900,000 people suffer with Parkinson's Disease

- 5,200,000 people suffer with Alzheimer's Disease

Just think, somewhere in your community, in your neighborhood, your church, your family- there is someone who needs you to –

- be a good listener to them

- cook them a healthy dinner

- do a load or 2 of laundry

- put fresh linens on their bed

- run errands for them

Good grief, the possibilities are endless . . .

So, Each Reach 1 - we can all do our part to make things a bit better, a bit brighter for those living day-by-day with degenerative neurological disease.

September 2, 2014

There's something so damned frightening about night - A vulnerability deep in the darkness, where time is held captive and emotions wince in desperation. Truth and awareness grow weary and worn in a battle for reflection of light. The mind's eye cannot find

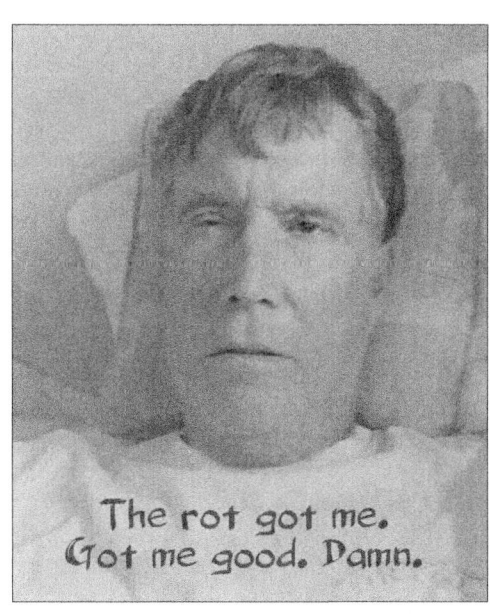

The rot got me.
Got me good. Damn.

focus, the horizon is lost. There are no points of reference. There can be no dead-reckoning without illumination.

And so, I wait, holding trust in tomorrow.

September 7, 2014

Yesterday found me in bed again. I'm getting more used to those days - they contrast the 'good' days', which I'm learning to appreciate more and more.

MSA has taught me some keen lessons:

- Learn to separate your ego from your purpose
- Beware of dangling carrots which threaten your contentment.
- Don't measure life as 'fair' or 'unfair' - a surfer's perfect wave

may ruin someone's sandcastle.

- Calculate risks - would you gamble $5,000 to win $20? Your choices in life may say otherwise.
- Conserve yourself - Allow time for healing and reflection, for direction and focus, for wisdom and grounding.
- Surrender all hope for a better yesterday
- Stop discarding the present for the lottery of tomorrow
- Celebrate experiences of joy and adversity
- Never take anything for granted
- Don't bark too much, share your toys, take naps
- Stop chasing your tail

September 8, 2014

The ability to imagine is the greatest gift one can have.

90

September 13, 2014

Ever wake up from one of those MSA 'power naps' and have no idea where you are? Or, if it's night or day? (which is especially confusing at dawn or dusk!) < YAWN >

September 18, 2014

- folks ask me, "How're ya doin'?"

Well, - I guess I'm doing as well as my old cell phone. I used to be a lot more useful, my battery no longer holds its charge, and I've lost some of my functions.

Or - maybe I'm more like a Slinky. Not really good for much, but some folks find it curious to watch me go down a set of stairs.

Wait - I'm somewhat like Scotland. Half of me struggles for my independence, while the other half worries about the future.

But - Like the sun and the moon and the tides, I always come 'round again . . . eventually!

October 2, 2014

- had a therapy session today to help soothe the emotions that this MSA rot exposes . . .and which covertly crawl onto the horizon of my dreams.

October 10, 2014

Let's pursue any links between traumatic brain injury, blunt head trauma, concussion, etc. and MSA.

October 15, 2014

I so appreciate my friends who are living with MSA, MS, Parkinson's, ALS and other neurological challenges - and the research and knowledge they share with me.

For the past 3+/- years, I have followed the Swank MSA Diet (although not always to the letter). It was recommended by my MS friends for whom is has worked well - and it has for me. I can actually 'feel' a change in my symptoms when I cheat for a few days! I try not to cheat - but, well....

Highly recommended by many folks these days is Dr. Perlmutter's work on brain health and food chemistry.

The question of exercise is ongoing. How much is appropriate, how to stay safe? Patients may be discouraged by treatment staff from exercising due to unstable blood pressure and the possibility of injury. When I was diagnosed, I was told to seek only 'movement therapy' - which is surely not aerobic. I've challenged that - but safety remains an issue for me. Most folks in local gyms have no idea what is appropriate for us. Hospital-based wellness centers may be a better choice. Be sure to explain your condition and the needs that arise. Remember, we overheat before we realize it - use caution.

Sleep. A serious problem for many of us. Our REM cycles are disrupted, and we may not get enough restorative sleep to avoid exhaustion. Sleep medications can be dangerous for us (check with your neurologist - whether it's a prescribed med, an over the counter product or a natural supplement). Lack of sleep manifests in very notable ways for us - and safety issues may increase. It's essential to discuss sleep issues with your treatment team - some issues are tied closely to breathing and the need for CPAP.

When we seek strategies and interventions to make our lives a bit better in the shadows of MSA, communication is essential. The research in degenerative neuro disease (MS> MSA, ALS, Parkinson's, etc.) often overlaps; we can learn so much by expanding our horizons and our understanding.

Is there a diet, a strategy, an intervention that has made a strong impact on you? Good news from any of us can become great news for all of us - Cheers!

October 16, 2014

Well, here it is after midnight - and I'm contemplating . . . "What are tremors good for?" Hmm. How about brushing your teeth? (no need for an electric toothbrush!). And stirring soup! (but not eating soup). Shaking hands! (even if it's all by yourself). Mastering smooth moves to an erratic rhythm, (even if no one else seems to feel them). Oh, and drawing squiggly lines! (just like your Dr) And, of course - staying awake, (especially when you badly need to sleep). It's like the "Red Shoes" - I can't stop dancin'! Now, say "Good night, Tremors." "Ok . . . good night, Tremors."

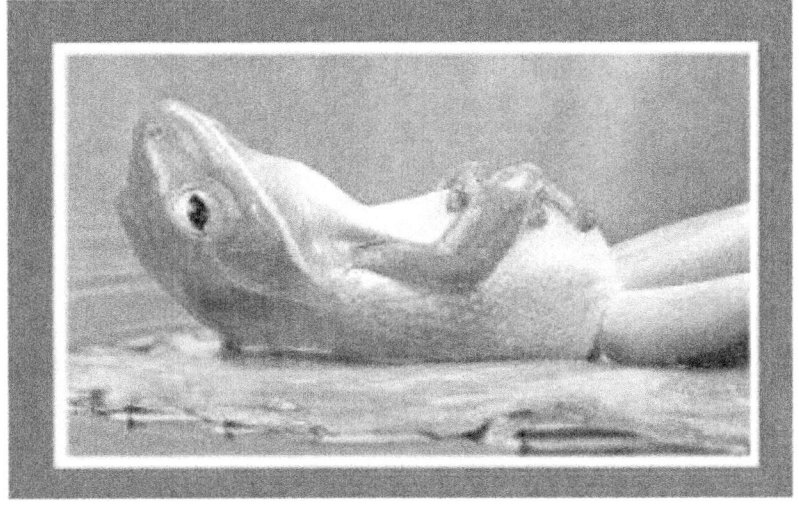

good day for a nap...

October 23, 2014

Hey gang! Sorry I've been absent from my post. Dean's away on business and I've had a bit of a bad run. But I now have a wonderful home-aid and a lovely little 'magic button' that I can press when I am alone and in desperate need. You know the sort - "Help, I've fallen, and I can't get up!"

I figure I'm soon to be a character with my own skits on Saturday Night LIVE . . . At any rate, I'm coming back around and headed in the right direction again. With any luck, I'll stay the course awhile-

November 15, 2014

Still awaiting word from my neurologist whether or not he will prescribe Rifampicin, despite the cancellation of the FDA study. I know I am slipping since I completed the year's study and dosage 5+ weeks ago. Maybe a 'pill clinic' will write a script? Ha! But I can enjoy eating again without discomfort - so, it's a nice break in that regard. Gee, sure didn't see this coming!

November 17, 2014

I bought 'Eventide' the day I received my diagnosis - upon leaving the neurologist's office, I headed straight to the docks where she lay. As I stood in her cockpit, I dreamed of crossing to West End, heading to Abacos or south to the Keys. Wind in my face, sun in my eyes . . .

It's been just over 4 years. We're both a bit older now, more worn; less able. I've had to adjust those dreams, as I've had to do with all the dreams I held in my early 50s. But, in their place, I've created new ones- dreams of healing and of hope for us all. And I've discovered that the joy in each moment is stronger than any dream I held for myself.

These days, when I'm able, I just sit aboard 'Eventide' and putter about. She seldom leaves the docks, although I bring her engines to a roar every so often. The power within them reminds me of the power within me.

November 18, 2014

Sometimes, I like to think of myself as Superman

- able to leap tall buildings,

- faster than a speeding bullet,

- more powerful than MSA!

But, when I'm most vulnerable, when MSA has reduced me to a point that

- I can barely move,

- I can barely eat,

- I can barely breathe,

- I don't feel much like a superhero.

In fact, I'm afraid. And I'm scared. I even cry. I know it will

96

pass, but I don't remember seeing Superman cry. I like to think even Clark Kent had moments of weakness. Now - Up, Up and Away!! (but where do I find a phone both these days?!)

December 19, 2014

Whew. Stress is doing me in. Yesterday, my car died. Today, I had to find a replacement. The gas company cut us off due to a bad meter. We've had no way to cook for 2 days. I am now reduced to a mass of tremors, spasms and cognitive impairment...almost in tears. But no. Chin up, peaceful thoughts. Onward!

December 20, 2014

This is a perfect time of year to remind ourselves to not become enslaved by our possessions,

- to not become indebted by them,
- to not allow our time to be consumed by them,
- to not allow them to alter our sense of values.

May we understand that the richness of life is measured with joy and contentment, with love of one another, with spiritual harmony, with acceptance.

December 23, 2014

" - settled my head for a long MSA nap . . ." Where does all my energy go these days? Maybe Santa will bring me more!

2015

January 3, 2015

Whatever happens in my life, I don't want to be defined by MSA.

It's only a thread in the tapestry, a brush stroke on the canvas.

It's part of the painting, not the frame.

January 13, 2015

Has MSA affected my cognition? My ability to process? My emotional response?

I must say, yes. It surely has. It's also changed my views. My perspective. My outlook. For the better.

January 17, 2015

Well, it's been 4 & 1/2 years since diagnosis and my annual neuro eval is this week. Things have changed in this past year:

- Breathing remains an issue. Friends and students often tell me I appear to be out of breath.
- My vision remains an issue. There are times, when I am tired, that I cannot keep my eyes open due to very high light sensitivity.

- Choking risks are quite high. I never eat alone and am careful to examine what I am eating to assist my swallowing. Water helps.

- My stamina is way down, Although I'm holding rather steady at one bedridden day a week, my 'active' hours daily have decreased. I require a great amount of 'recharging'.

- Cognitive and emotional processing is impaired. I cannot react automatically - I must stop and concentrate on issues and situations.

Otherwise, I find myself enveloped in stress and anxiety. But, on the other side of the coin, I am still viable. I'm able to reach out and bring meaning and purpose into my days. And for that, I am grateful!

January 21, 2015

This is my 'happy, post-neuro eval report'. Progression of the disease appears to have slowed overall . . . although a few symptoms have advanced a bit. Overall, the greatest bit was receiving an improved prognosis (although, I've taken all that with a salt crystal).

It also looks like I might be getting professional support/assistance for data*MSA. Fine day.

I get by with a little help from my friends.

February 13, 2015

The day after a 'lost day' (24+ hours bedridden) is always challenging. I must push myself to get going, even though I really don't feel up to it.

All my systems are in some sort of recovery; respiration, circulation, digestion, vision, cognition, fine and gross motor skills - it's a cornucopia of dysfunction!

So today, I got up and got going . . . Bit by bit, I pushed my systems to get up to snuff. They kept pushing back . . .hard.

But it's Friday the 13th - what can possibly go wrong?

Mar 3, 2015

I was rollin' along pretty good this morning . . . but, soon after this snapshot, something spun me around a full 180 degrees. I quickly found my systems shut down, which left me bedridden for the next 5 hours. MSA: mysterious symptoms abound!

Lady the Wonderdog brings me comfort.

March 7, 2015

Were you ever up on a high ladder and your foot slipped from the next rung, and suddenly everything seemed uncertain and a bit frightening? That's life with MSA. - after tests this morning, here's what I know: there's a lot I don't know!

Still awaiting word on the transient ischemic attack (TIA) screening from the doctor. Likely, not the issue - I heard the tech say "clean" to another tech. Maybe, she was asking her to clean something. Who knows?

All blood work came back fine. Very slight dehydration - but, with MSA, it could be enough to trigger a sequence of events. Heart good, lungs good, brain…well, hmm?

Now, enough of doctors and stroke-like episodes - I have schools to visit!

gotta remember!
date: 10/03/15   M Tu W Th F (Sa) Su

top 5 list *for World MSA Day! (multiple system atrophy)*

1 *learn more about MSA through:* www.multiplesystematrophy.org ☐
2 *share MSA infor with my drs. to make them more aware* ☐
3 *learn about MSA patient experiences:* www.dataMSA.com ☐
4 *make a donation toward neuro-research* ☐
5 *stay in touch with the latest MSA updates year-round* ☐
6 *become an MSA-Pal to someone affected* ☐

✓ *don't forget...everyone can make a difference*

dataMSA.com

March 12, 2015

MSA Awareness Month tip:

We should remember that most MSA patients live with the condition for a few years or more before receiving a diagnosis.

We tend to refer to the amount of time since our diagnosis- in my case, 4.5 years- but that fails to represent the timeline accurately. My neurologist thinks I've been living with MSA for approximately 7 years . . .some days, it seems like much more!

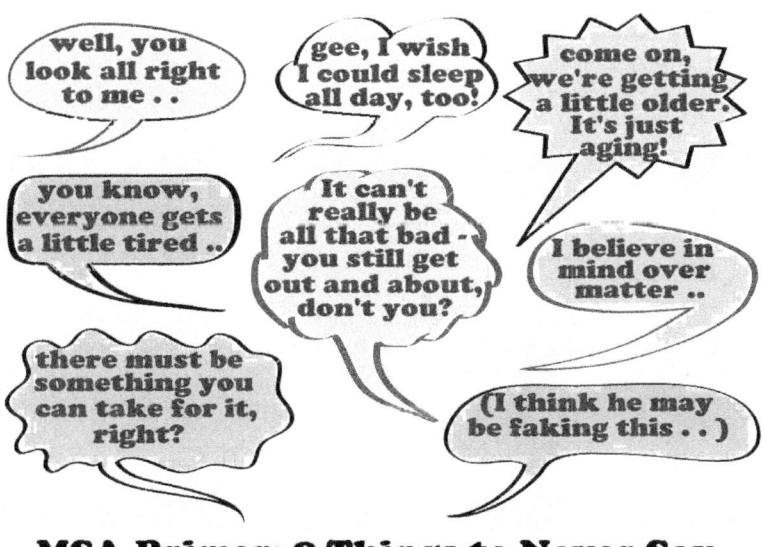

MSA Primer: 8 Things to Never Say (never!)

dataMSA.com

March 29, 2015

When this MSA rot holds me bedbound for hours on end, and I go into periods of deep sleep -my brain goes a bit wild! I have very vivid and colorful dreams - very detailed, but not at all frightening. It's as though I experience a chemical 'flush' of some sort.

I actually don't mind it a bit! It brings some entertainment into the mix...

April 1, 2015

10 years ago, today -I almost lost my life to an abdominal bleed. I had lost nearly 70% of my blood internally and was within a breath of dying.

Luckily, a quick response team and skilled surgeons saved me along with a stint, 33 staples and weeks in ICU/CCU.
I was temporarily paralyzed on my right side - but recovered quickly. Those who know me well know the spiritual experiences that accompanied this.

So, MSA be damned. I am a survivor! And that's no foolin'.

May 5, 2015

Hope you're having some fun today - and, if you are, have some for me! Three days down. Damn. . . I have things to do, places to go and people to annoy....

May 18, 2015

Yesterday afternoon, something went terribly, terribly wrong. I had a rather strong morning, ran a few errands, and met friends for lunch. Everything seemed fine.

But, by approx. 3p, I started to suffer cognitive failure. I suddenly lost a good bit of my memory regarding names, places and vocabulary. Within an hour or so, as I fought to recover, an extreme headache overcame me - affecting the left frontal lobe and Broca's area. The pain was crippling.

Foolishly, I refused to get to the hospital. After another hour or so, I was able to get to sleep. When I awoke, many hours later, I had fully recovered my functioning, although a dull headache remained.

I hope to see my doctors this morning; it was a frightening situation. MSA? Who knows? Maybe, I'll find out.

I have a feeling that my brain now looks something like this.

dataMSA.com

May 19, 2015

More tests tomorrow bright and early. . .. well, early. TIA screening, just to rule it out because this episode has occurred 2x in 2 years. The deeper suspicion is MSA complications and resulting autonomic failure in circulation, blood pressure, blood vessel dilation, yada yada.

What an odd path we MSA folks walk . . . when we are able to walk a tall!

June 4, 2015

These days, whenever I'm strong enough, I enjoy volunteering in our local schools. After nearly 25 years in Education, it's in my blood . . .

Occasionally, when I'm on campus, I'm reminded by colleagues of statements made by a co-worker back when I was undergoing neurological assessments for my MSA symptoms. She apparently believed I was 'faking all of it to get out of work'. She must have felt so strongly about her beliefs that she went as high as my Director with her opinions.

Perhaps, I should take comfort in the fact that she did offer to pray for me.

At this point, with all I am facing, this really shouldn't bother me. But - it does. It brought a very bitter end to an otherwise enjoyable and rewarding career.

We each have a responsibility to be thoughtful in our words, our actions, our deeds- recklessness by one can be devastating to another . . .

June 11, 2015

Last night, I fell asleep with the TV on. It must have been a crime show because I began thinking about my MSA diagnosis:

- "circumstantial evidence"
- "reasonable doubt"
- "life sentence without parole"

Maybe, it was because of this latest research on possible causes for MSA. Who knows? But what if I have something else? Something that could be treated or cured?

106

Do I have to play this hand, or can I trade for other cards are in the deck?

It's fun to dream ….

June 19, 2015

Well, I did it! I wore myself out! Everything shifted quickly- vision, balance, breathing, stamina. Good thing my bed was close by!

June 29, 2015

Today is tough - Dean is just starting to pull out of pneumonia, and I've been in bed with MSA rot since Saturday am. My legs are uncooperative, my breathing is off . . .but I have a meeting in a few hours with the museum regarding my children's book.

July 4, 2015

Boy, the nights can be hard . . .hard physically, hard emotionally. I sometimes feel like a golf ball cut open.

July 8, 2015

Five years ago this week I received my diagnosis of MSAp and a prognosis of 66-72 months. Dean and I cried a bit in the neuro's office, then I firmly stated, "Nope, I'll outlive that." The doctor said, "I hope you do . . . "

So far, so good. Diet, exercise, attitude, faith, luck - I mix them all together and get on with life, each moment, each hour, day by day,

Thanks, my friends, for being there with me.

July 13, 2015

Well, the Summer of '15 isn't all beach balls and bar-b-que . . .Two lovely new symptoms have made themselves known - 1) spasms that rock me, mostly in my back, hips, neck - 2) a hollowness in my chest followed by lightheadedness.

I'll visit Dr. Neuro to learn more - but, in the meantime- Surf's Up!

July 18, 2015

Today I choked like I've never choked before. And I've choked many times before.

Scared the *&%# out of me. Get the blender ready.

July 26, 2015

Sometimes, with this rot, I become so angry, so afraid, I want to

- pound 10penny nails into a 2x4
- demolish cinder blocks with a sledgehammer
- chop logs with a hand axe
- dig holes and refill them again

I want to

- break dinner plates on my kitchen floor
- drive my car on the highway and scream into the night
- cry where no one can hear me

I want to

- lie on the beach and talk to the stars
- get lost in the woods and talk to the trees
- climb the green foothills and talk to God

But, instead, I get on with my day as best I can -I want to appreciate how lucky I am.

August 12, 2015

Last night, my brain shorted out. I mean, shorted out more than usual. I felt like I was seeing the Northern Lights in my mind's eye - and there was no 'off' switch.

Actually, it was beautifully entertaining but, it soon grew too intense and irritating.... eventually, though, I must have fallen asleep.

I love how my brain works - I just wish I had a little more control over it. I guess it's an analogy of life!

August 13, 2015

Lately, I've been operating with a sense of urgency- taking on more than usual, pushing harder. I've engaged myself in key projects and purposeful 'missions', each with distinct timelines and charted courses.

I strongly sense I must do what I can while I can, a nebulous boundary of will and ability, an invisible struggle within the self to maintain control.

I'm up against the mutinous crew of MSA.

September 8, 2015

When an MSA 'cycle' is beginning, I have trouble with my eyes and my breathing becomes labored. I experience chills regardless of the temperature and my movements slow.

Time to hunker down with Lady the Wonderdog to ride it out....

September 11, 2015

With school back in session, I thought I'd give myself a very basic MSA Progress Report for the past year.

(>)= increased, (<)= decreased, (-) no noticeable change

Here goes:

Breathing difficulty = (>)

Choking = (>)

Confusion/Memory Issues = (>)

Digestive issues = (-)

Emotionality = (>)

Falls = (<)

Fatigue = (>>)

Mobility = (-)

Sleep disorder = (-)

Tremors = (-)

Vision issues = (>)

Overall, it's not too bad!

September 19, 2015

Changes with MSA come from the inside, out. By the time anyone notices things are different, things have been different for quite a while. Folks don't have to say anything to make us feel better - just be aware, accommodating, kind - and patient. Very patient. We're not quite the persons we used to be.

September 22, 2015

I've wondered why I've been irritated lately. Impatient. Compelled. Then, I realized that 63 months ago, I received a prognosis of 66-72 months. I didn't buy into it then, nor do I now, but on the days I really struggle, it sticks a bit.

October 5, 2015

Had a check-up with my GP today...I've been seeing him for 15+ years. He lost his father to MSA a few years back. It's wonderful to be able to have frank discussions with someone who understands.

He reported that his father fought the good fight and was stubborn as a mule throughout it all. His father's experiences inspired me to push myself pretty hard today.

October 20, 2015

push, push, push, push...VICTORY!

nap, nap, nap, nap.... Zzzzzz

October 22, 2015

I'm back at my desk to do some writing and Lady in the background, is watching passersby out the window. Nice South Florida day here. Yesterday was wicked rough. I needed assistance in every aspect of living skills. Thank goodness, Dean stayed home from work.

I can tell when a bad spell is coming- my eyes water and become terribly sensitive. My breathing shallows and labors. My motor skills begin to fail; swallowing is difficult. I feel chills, regardless of the temperature.

From there, it's the next stage. My eye will not open properly, my breathing remains very difficult and I become nearly totally immobile. My mind and my thinking are still sharp, but even talking can be challenging. I develop spasms and muscle cramps. Toileting is affected. I cannot eat. I try to swallow liquids and very soft food, but it's tough. I lie in bed and let the hours pass. The fatigue is insurmountable.

After several hours of this, I can feel my brain struggling to reboot. It can take anywhere from 12- 70+ hours before I can walk, eat, and so forth. Then, I slowly climb out into the next phase, recovery.

During recovery, all systems are a bit off. But they gradually return to a state of normalcy. Some system functions take much longer to recover than others. The fatigue remains and I stay close to home because I can, and sometimes do regress, in this stage. Recovery usually takes 8-10 hours. Then, I am able to function again!

This cycle repeats irregularly. However, it's generally 1x every 7-10 days and can consume up to 3 days. Sometimes, I pull out after 2. I chart these spells for duration and frequency; I've been holding steady for a while (knock wood).

So, there you have it. A snapshot of my Living Day by Day with MSA!

November 2, 2015

Today, I felt like cheap aluminum foil I looked a lot like others- a shiny side, a duller side. It seemed like I was up to the job, but as soon as I was stressed the smallest bit, I proved I wasn't up to the task...Can I be recycled?

November 12, 2015

When I began working with children with special needs, I worked with 2 young men with brain injury: one the result of a car accident, the other a gunshot victim.

Their therapy focused on utilizing the plasticity of the brain to develop new neuro pathways and bypass damaged areas to improve fine/gross motor skills and cognition. It was in many ways successful, due in part to their young ages.

I've been implementing those strategies for myself for several months in dealing with MSA. Although my damage is organic rather than traumatic, I reasoned the process is much the same. I attempt to bypass damaged areas to utilize healthy cells, thereby reducing effects. Of course, I don't have youth on my side, but I do have determination.

It's a multi-faceted approach, utilizing pyscho-social, cognitive and physical stimulation/challenges. In a few words, I push myself to retain failing abilities while challenging myself to learn new skills. And I know when to pull back on the throttle for rest and recovery.

As a result, the cycles of my 'lost days' have not changed, I still face 1-2 days bedridden out of every 7-10. During those periods, I continue to experience many system failures. These cycles have held fairly steady for the past 6 months.

Overall, my energy levels appear slightly higher - but I still require a great deal of rest daily.

However, my mobility, my fine and gross motor skills and my task completion levels are markedly improved. My doctors report that the progression of MSA-related effects appears to have slowed and they are pleased with the outcomes.

I plan to continue this approach with the hope of utilizing undamaged brain cells at a rate that outpaces MSA progression. It's become a competition. Stay tuned!

MY HOME HEALTH AID, LADY

November 29, 2015

Some of you have asked how I am doing in my approach to retrain this old brain. I've been applying techniques I learned years ago when I worked with brain-injured children.

In summary, when I struggle with a task, I redirect/distract my brain, then attempt the task again. The hope is to prompt the brain to seek/develop new pathways.

Yesterday was a true test. My motor skills were shot, and my breathing was labored; I was totally consumed by fatigue. It typically would have been what I call a 'lost day', one spent in bed hour upon hour.

I applied my technique by distracting my brain from the tasks at hand. I tried television and conversation. Neither worked. In desperation, I managed to place both feet on the ground and focused on sensory feedback...touch, sound, and so forth. Then,

I set off. Wasn't at all easy... but I got going-and kept going. The sense of fatigue never abated, but I was able to function.

I'm not sure if this approach is working or if it's just odds/coincidence working in my favor, but I'm going to keep at it. My hope is that by stimulating and pushing my motor skills, my autonomic systems, in their effort to keep up, will also seek unblocked pathways.

If we only use a percentage of the brain for our daily activities, there are dormant areas to tap into... I should add the importance of careful diet and appropriate exercise.

I'll keep you posted. Here's hoping hope for us all!

December 18, 2015

As many who follow me know, I've been applying basic concepts of neuroplasticity and 'neuro-tuning' to enhance day by day functioning.

The concepts implement strategies to develop new neural pathways, with the goal of bypassing damaged cells. I implement cognitive behavioral interventions to help employ the strategies.

Of course, this model serves to attempt restructuring of neural transmission and cannot in any way be viewed as treatment of the disease itself. At this point, there may be notable benefits. Some gross motor skills appear to have improved, increasing mobility. Falls are greatly reduced; balance has improved. I require a cane much less and can walk farther. Stamina has increased, as a result. Some fine motor skills appear to have improved, including the ability to use utensils, handle tools, and hand write.

Employing yoga techniques of relaxation, deep breathing and focus, appears to have improved breathing abilities. Respiration appears to be more moderated, with reduced episodes of shortness of breath. However, chewing and swallowing have worsened a bit and choking remains a high risk. Tuning of these skill sets is ongoing.

Although I journal the strategies, timeline and outcomes it's surely not a scientifically sound model. For me, it's a race to build neural pathways faster than the disease can disable them. I'll keep you posted!

December 22, 2015

One small, slightly stressful event can send me into a tailspin. Breathing goes wonky, motor skills fail. I feel lightheaded and daft. Good thing this time of year brings no stressful events!

December 23, 2015

Last night, I was on the rocks. My peanut brain completed shorted out. My senses overloaded, my breathing and pulse raced- it wasn't a good feeling at all. I kept waiting for the calm of dawn.

2016

January 4, 2016

For the next few days, I'll be posting information about my implementing some concepts of neural training- and my rationale for doing so. Any of this, of course, cannot be viewed as a cure or treatment; nothing I have done is 'scientifically sound'. Rather, I want to share some of the strategies that have improved my day to day life. Just my perspective after 5 years...

But I'd like to start with the importance of good diet. In the past, I've followed popular diets, the MS diet and Dr. Perlmutter's diets. I found neither to bring about notable changes after giving each a 6-month implementation period, although each has invaluable advice.

Overall, I have found some specific diet choices to be effective. Here are some observations I've made in the years I've been wrestlin' with this MSA rot:

a) cut out all artificial sweeteners, no matter how 'natural' they claim to be. Either use a bit of sugar or do without. I generally do without.

b) no soft drinks, especially diet (see above). There is no redeeming value in them, and they throw your system off for quite a while.

c) no highly processed foods. If you can't read the ingredients, don't eat it. It's difficult to avoid processed foods altogether, but frozen entrees, deserts, snacks and fast foods must be examined carefully. Be alert to sodium, as well!

d) simple is better! Better to eat a well-prepared soup than something from a can or frozen food section. Fresh vegetables, fresh fruit, freshly prepared grains. Not difficult to do.

e) meat is important (for me at, least), but in moderation. Never a serving more than the size of your palm. I try to limit red meat to 2-3 servings a week. Chicken, a bit more. Remember to trim excess fat. Sadly, I despise seafood, but it's an excellent choice.

g) Use sense with butter. Real butter is a better choice than margarine and artificial products. Again, moderation.

h) Avoid sweets. Sounds like something your mom might say, but it's good advice. If you must indulge, do so in the early afternoon rather than at night. I find complex carbs before bed render me restless and, later, listless. Although yogurt and fruit are a good choice, many yogurts are very high in added sugar (and other stuff!). Go natural.

i). Little to no alcohol. Some may argue this- I can only speak from my experiences. Alcohol makes my wee brain short out. It's very uncomfortable.

j) I use a boost of caffeine to get me going in the morning. It helps. I add no sugar (I prefer organic teas to coffee). However, no caffeine after noon (loosely). It restricts blood vessels and over-stimulates systems. And then, there are the related sleep disorders....

h) Everything in moderation, including moderation. I don't stick to any one plan any longer...it was just too difficult. Instead, I make sensible decisions. If I want to eat bacon, I eat 1/2 a slice. If I want a chocolate bar, I take a small piece. Maybe a half glass of Coke on a hot day once in a great while. You get the idea. Don't keep things in your cupboards that are going to tempt you!

Tomorrow, I'll discuss how, after the Rifampicin clinical trial, probiotics changed my health and wellbeing - and some of the science behind it. Be well!

January 5, 2016

Yesterday, as a lead in to how the concepts of neuro-training have (+) impacted my life, I discussed a bit about diet. Just a bit.

Today's topic links diet to neural health. A few years back, I participated in the 1-year clinical trial for Rifampin/Rifampicin, studied for potentially slowing the progression of MSA. This was a double-blind study, so none of us 100 folks knew if we had the drug or a placebo. For me, it became clear rather quickly.

By the end of the 3rd month, I was having a hard time digesting certain food...especially meats and dairy products. By the 6- month point, it was all rather uncomfortable. The clinical trial drs. wanted to pull me out, but I insisted on going forward. By the close of my study, I resisted eating anything but certain vegetables and rice. It wasn't much fun at all...to make it worse, the drug proved to be ineffective in the treatment of MSA (however, I'm not certain about that- more later).

It was at that point I began taking probiotics. Within months, the combination of the probiotics and the ceasing of high doses of Rifampin brought me around. I began to feel better in and about the gut than I had prior to the study. I kept on taking the probiotics and never looked back.

We see a lot these days about probiotic health...much more than I can possibly write here. Suffice it to say, for those of us over 50, you cannot get enough probiotic infusion from yogurt and other foods that claim to boost gut health. All sorts of celebrities are selling us a bill of goods on that matter, stating they feel like they're in their 30s because of Greek yogurt!

But more important is the connection between our digestive health and our neural health. This connection has been known for decades - read The Second Brain by M. Gershon. The bulk of serotonin neurotransmitters is created in our gut...only a small percentage are created by the brain.

Our gut controls an amazing amount of our overall health. A lack of good digestive health can greatly impact all nervous system functioning, affecting both autonomic nerve effector junctions and skeletal neuromuscular effector junctions. This has been studied and validated.

So, probiotic health is essential. But to be effective, probiotics must work with food. No probiotic supplement will work if there isn't adequate nutritional chemistry to respond to. Page back to the discussion on healthy diet. Eat well, take probiotics... essential if you're going to fight symptoms of MSA.

But which probiotic supplement? There are countless varieties on the market, each claiming to be better than the next. I surely haven't the credentials to make claims about one over another, so I'll say this: Discuss your choices with your doctors, your pharmacist, your neurologist to get informed opinions. Then, get on board!

With diet choices under control and a healthy probiotic system, we take one giant step forward to reduce the impact of

MSA. Tomorrow, I'll introduce my personal neural training techniques.

As I have always stated, nothing I propose should be seen as a cure or treatment - I am hoping to share my successes as I wander through this rot. Be healthy!

January 6, 2016

My recent posts about creating and maintaining overall wellness were to be accompanied tonight by a bit on perseverance...then I wound up in bed all day today. Maybe we'll table perseverance for now! Meanwhile –

In my late adolescence, I volunteered to work with children with disabilities (and later studied to become an ESE teacher). Two of the boys I worked with at the time suffered from brain injury, one from a car accident, the other from an accidental gunshot (I could write volumes about that alone).

Because they were young, much of their treatment focused on 'brain plasticity'. I was just a teen-aged volunteer, but I was fascinated with the concepts and strategies attempted.

These many years later, I don't know how well either boy eventually recovered, but I did see progress in the time I was with them. Fast forward to a few years ago - facing MSA debilitation, I found myself revisiting those experiences. I wondered if there were significant differences in brain damage brought about by traumatic injury and brain damage brought about by disease, like MSA, etc.

Reading and research lead me to explore concepts of neural training, a science which employs brain plasticity to enhance and rebuild skills. A great deal has been written about this over the span of decades, mostly with regards to traumatic brain injury (TBI). However, a few articles discussed implementation with Parkinson's patients.

From my MSA diagnosis in July 2010 to this point, I have remained as active as I possibly can. I knew, from my ESE experiences, it was essential to maintain what I could for as long as I could.

Although age was not on my side with regard to brain plasticity, I began to employ basic neural training techniques. I noticed that some strategies appeared to help. While most of the gains are neuromuscular, I have also seen slight changes in autonomic functioning. Remember, this is based only on my observations, as I struggle to stay ahead of MSA progression.

More on this important topic later...for this night, though, it's back to bed. Be well,

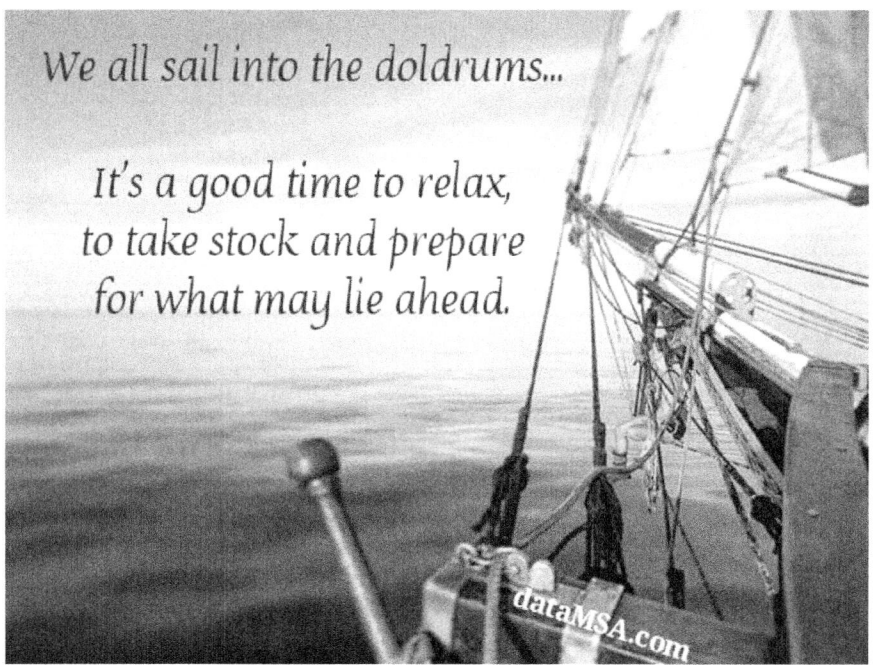

We all sail into the doldrums...

It's a good time to relax, to take stock and prepare for what may lie ahead.

January 7, 2016

Ok... as promised- a bit about neuroplasticity. This is a weighty topic, so what I present here skims the surface. I'm hopeful, though, it will be enough to convey the concepts.

The easiest way to think of neuroplasticity is to see it as re-learning. The brain relies on the same basic neurobiological processes it used to acquire skills initially, but through new neural pathways. As a result, there are two ways improvement may occur: recovery and compensation.

Recovery includes:

-Restoration of neural tissue

-Restoration of movement

-Restoration of activity

Compensation refers to:

-Recruitment of new neural circuits (neural level)

-Training of new movement sequences (behavioral level)

-Training of activity in a new way (activity level)

In summary, recovery relates to restoration of lost functions; compensation relates to the acquisition of new functions to replace those lost.

Because our brains have a large capacity for redundancy, there are areas of the brain that respond to the same stimuli and therefore can create new neural pathways.

By challenging ourselves, we can improve our neuro-functioning through brain plasticity. Changes in our behavior or experiences result in changes on a neurobiological level. Simply stated, if we increase an activity, we can increase the related synapses. Conversely, if we reduce or stop an activity, we reduce and may eventually lose those related synapses. The difference becomes prolonged independence vs. hastened dependence.

Think of neuroplasticity as an ongoing a state that has existed from our prenatal and postnatal neurodevelopment to the many changes our brains undergo from our life's experiences (including changes to our brain brought about by MSA).

It's known that our experiences shape and mold our brains completely - through the neurochemicals, the axons and dendrites, the maps and cortical networks. I'm hopeful that through neuroplasticity we can create experiences that can restore some of our brain functions so we may stay a few steps ahead of the effects of MSA.

Later on, I'll discuss the specific interventions I employ. Be healthy!

Don't measure your journey against someone else's horizon.

dataMSA.com

January 8, 2016

Today was a good one for me! Let me share with you how I adapt the concepts of neuroplasticity and neural training...I'll start tonight with 'redirection', an intervention for neuromuscular recovery. When I am faced with a task that I am struggling with (or, if task-related tremors present strong interference), I redirect my brain away from the task to something that incorporates unrelated skills. Then, after a brief period of time, I return to the intended task.

For example, I often experience tremors when I attempt to use a fork or spoon - or when I attempt handwriting. The tremors can interfere to the point that the task cannot be accomplished. Our instincts may compel us to work through the task, in spite of the obstacles...a 'keep at it' approach. However, one might think of this as driving into a cul-de-sac and hoping to get to the other side of the neighborhood by continuing to approach the cul-de-sac over and over again.

In the case of the working/task related tremors, I redirect my processes. I put the utensil down and employ a completely different task. I may engage in conversation, walk across the room, pet the dog. Anything at all that will distract the brain and pull it out of the cul-de-sac.

After about 20-30 seconds, I reattempt the original task (in this case, using the utensil). Of course, I may see no change at all, but I repeat the process. I will do this 3-4 times, even if there is no sign of change.

The principle is to retrain the brain to seek an unobstructed pathway, to seek a neural pathway that may be redundant and is capable of completing the task. Results do not come quickly; I must attempt this strategy many times over and for each obstructive behavior.

After several months of employing this procedure, I see (+) results in 2 primary neuromotor skills, working tremors in my hands and my ability to walk (more on that later). However, I regress quickly when confronted with any stressful situation in which I must react quickly. I may assume that in those instances, I return to the original and likely damaged neuropathway.

All of the plasticity interventions that I have been employing are used in collaboration with one another. Later, I will discuss one that seems to run counter to redirection. Stay tuned!

And remember, these are only my experiences, and are based on my reading and research. Not an exact science, not a cure. Just hoping to cope a bit better and stay ahead of the progression. Be well.

When the sea presents challenges, hunker down and sail on...

dataMSA.com

January 9, 2016

In yesterday's post, I discussed the principles of 'redirection' as it relates to neural training. Redirection is one of the tools I've been employing to increase neuromotor functioning. But, what about strategies for autonomic system recovery?

One example is the lack sensitivity I experience(d) in both feet (primarily the left) and both hands. These symptoms grew worse as MSA progressed, causing numbness and clumsiness.

Using a brain plasticity concept involving differentiated stimulation, I sought to utilize redundant neuro pathways in hopes of restoring sensory nerve functioning (differentiated stimulation utilizes a variety of stimuli and variable duration).

I used a pumice stone to sensitize both feet and forced stimulation by, at various times, walking barefoot on sand, asphalt, grass and so forth. I also bought a shower mat with a course and somewhat prickly texture. I used massage often to encourage neuro transmission.

I employed similar techniques to restore the sensitivity in my fingertips, which had deteriorated to the point it was difficult for me to handle items such as utensils. I set out some bolts, nuts and washers of various sizes and practiced assembling and disassembling to encourage tactile stimulation through fine motor skills.

After several months of these strategies, I began to see (+) results. I can report that much sensitivity has returned to both feet and both hands.

A second example of my use of differentiated stimulation focuses on perspiration. About 2.5 years ago, I noticed that I no longer perspired properly. Perspiration, if it occurred at all, was delayed and the rate of perspiration was low. For my safety, I began avoiding situations in which overheating could put me at risk, which was difficult in south Florida.

Realizing that this condition was worsening and that I was losing this critical function, I began to employ differentiated stimulation by attempting to force myself to sweat.

With some modicum of safety, I began exposing myself to small amounts of heat, followed by a cooling shower. A bit more heat, another cooling, and so forth. I did this a few times a week, eventually lengthening the sessions slightly and increasing frequency (when it was safe to do so).

After months of employing this strategy, I observed I was perspiring more... and more quickly. Continuing with the implementation brought (+) results. Today, I may be at near total recovery in this autonomic and essential function. I may be... time will tell.

Success in both examples may focus on the plasticity of the brain to seek and employ redundant pathways. However, these are my observations based solely on my experiences and research. Although I am quite pleased with the results, I can in no way provide validity or reliability to the techniques used.

I am employing other neuro plasticity strategies, in addition to redirection and differentiated stimulation, which I will share a bit later. Be well!

January 11, 2016

During the past week, I've shared some of the research I've done on brain plasticity and neural training. These strategies are most often used with persons with TBI (traumatic brain injury) and stroke, but after reviewing related material I couldn't reason why the strategies wouldn't work for a person with organic damage, such as MSA. So, 18 month ago, I created a treatment plan for myself. So far, so good.

There are still some system issues I've been unable to affect, such as swallowing. And tremors. My breathing still goes wonky at times and on and on. And then there's fatigue....

Early into my diagnosis, periods of debilitating fatigue came 1x/14 days and would last for 8-10 hours. The cycles began increasing in both duration and frequency. Eventually, I was experiencing them 1x/7 days for up to 70 hours.

My neuro docs weren't sure what was causing it but explained that it could be a result of the brain healing in some way... perhaps new neuropathways were created during these periods. Maybe it was a good thing.

However, as I collected and reviewed patient information via the dataMSA surveys, I observed that cycles of this sort tend to grow both in frequency and duration. I charted my days carefully to see if there were changes. Then, it dawned on me: What if the doctors are wrong? What if these cycles have nothing whatsoever to do with healing? Should I be fighting the fatigue? Perhaps I was giving in too easily. 70+ hours in bed every 7-10 days is not natural, nor is it healthy.

I rationalized that this sort of fatigue is artificial in nature. That is to say not brought about by any true sort of exhaustion. When the cycles presented and I felt I could barely function, I managed to get my feet to touch the floor. I took time to catch my breath, then pushed. I got up and moved. I stumbled to a chair or the sofa. I sat for a while, then, I got up and moved again. And again. And again.

In early attempts, I could only keep going for a half hour before I wound up back in bed. But I didn't stay there. I pushed more. I got up and repeated the process.

To date, the results are good. I still need rest (nap-snacks, I call them) and the cycles still present themselves. I don't always feel like pushing back ...but I do. As a result, my stamina has increased. I am more viable...and more hopeful.

Neural training seems to be working for me. Since we cannot effectively chart deterioration of the brain, I must assume MSA is still progressing. But my goal is to activate and utilize healthy neuro tissue, to increase neurotransmission and to outpace the advancement of MSA.

I'll be creating a survey on dataMSA, which will focus on patient responses to these strategies. You may be using them now. Let's share our outcomes to encourage others.

Meanwhile, remember to stay as healthy and fit as you can. It matters a great deal in all of this. Be well.

January 16, 2016

This past week, I shared some of the strategies I've used to improve my stance against this MSA rot, including diet, pre and probiotics, activity and neural training activities. But I forgot something important: socialization.

Often, folks with debilitating conditions avoid socializing. We may fear not being able to 'keep up' or we may be experiencing voice issues. At times, we fear being overstimulated. But socialization is essential.

With regards to neuroplasticity and neural training, socialization is a great exercise. It isn't always easy, even with friends and family, because it takes nearly every part of the brain to interact with others. We must read social cues by listening to what people say and how they say it. We must also observe and track details of facial expressions.

A bit of science...the fusiform gyrus, located near the base of our brain, is involved in seeing face while the occipital cortex helps us observe others. Of course, we must also tune in to voices. An entire neural network, involving both hemispheres, is devoted to language and how we decipher the ways in which people add layers of meaning to their spoken words.

I know there are many who aren't able do this, but we each must do what we can to engage healthy neuropathways and encourage skill retention and enhancement.

I surely can't find the cure for MSA, but I do hope I can inspire others to adopt concepts of neuroplasticity to improve their quality of life with MSA.

January 20, 2016

Yesterday I didn't follow my own advice -I woke up in an MSA fog and decided I would return to bed for a few minutes. A few minutes stretched into an hour. Then two.

I knew it would be good for me to fight back, to get up and try to move about. To try to walk a little. But I was a coward. Somehow, the safety of the bed won out over me trying to overcome. I sought the sanctuary of the blankets.

So, two hours became an entire day. By the time I did get up, my walking was very poor, my swallowing was terrible, my eyes were wonky. I was a mess. I let the rot get the best of me. As Kip said in Napoleon Dynamite, "I'm just kinda P. O. 'd..."

Today was different. I got up and pushed. And pushed. And pushed. By noon, I was pretty tired. But it was a good tired. I needed a nap and I took one. Then, I got up and kept at it.

Tomorrow, I'm going to share my thoughts on treatment planning for us MSA folk - stay tuned!

TO STAY ALOFT, DREAM ABOUT WHAT LIES JUST OVER THE HORIZON.

dataMSA.com

January 25, 2016

In the past couple of weeks, I've been sharing some of my research and applications regarding neural training/brain plasticity. I'd like to continue by discussing Personal Treatment Planning (PTP).

As a teacher for students with special needs, I was expected to develop an IEP (individualized educational plan) for each of my students. This plan brought together all of the

134

academic and social factors needed to encourage success and remove obstacles to learning.

I believe those of us with MSA should employ something quite similar - a PTP, to encourage ourselves toward better living, day by day. I'd like to begin this concept by discussing 'baseline data'.

It's rather hard to know if we're making much headway with neural training and other strategies if we aren't quite certain of our starting point. Of course, most of us know our limitations - but do we know our successes?

If you're not already doing so, consider keeping a journal or log of your most notable MSA symptoms. Using a scale of 1-10, rate the severity and then track the duration of symptoms. If you find this overwhelming, you may want to focus on 2 or 3 symptoms in particular - we might consider these 'target symptoms'.

I chose to collect information daily (sometimes twice daily) on the following:
- mobility (how far I could walk, how often, and whether or not I needed assistance),
- debilitating fatigue and bed rest (how often it occurred and how long it lasted),
- insomnia/sleep disorder (how often it occurred and the duration of sleep).
- I also tracked choking incidents when they happened.

By following this model for at least one month, we can begin to understand the baseline of our symptoms. As we introduce interventions, such as neural training, we can measure signs of progress by continuing the charting.

Yes, this does take some time. And it may be a bit depressing at first. But with consistent application, it can also signal hope and promise that interventions are having (+) effects. Of course, as I always stress, this is not a cure of any kind, but rather a way to develop a higher level of functioning.

More on this later. In the meanwhile, stay warm- and don't let foul weather prevent you from essential exercise, activity and good diet!

February 1, 2016

FYI: 66 months ago, I received a prognosis of 66-72 months. 48 months ago, I was told I would need to acquire a wheelchair. I was also told I'd need to stop driving. But I refused to sell my cars, or my boat. I refused to believe that there was no hope. I decided to fight in any way I could. Today, I walked a half mile. On the beach. In the sand. Then, I drove home.

If you've been following this page, you know that I research and apply principles of neural training/brain plasticity. You may refer to previous posts for the details. Recently, I've discussed the benefits of preparing a 'personal treatment plan' (PTP) to frame purposeful intervention. While we cannot cure this MSA rot ourselves, we may be able to outrun it for a while. In prior posts, I discussed the importance of diet & probiotic strategies for neuro health. Tonight, I'd like to discuss how we may apply neuro training techniques into the exercise component of our PTPs.

REDIRECTION: When we attempt a physical activity, we may find that we're 'blocked' - that we may tremor/spasm badly, or we may be unable to bring forth the motor skills needed to complete the task. The concept of redirection guides us to distract ourselves from the 'failing' task, rather than forcing ourselves into a 'cul de sac'. Try another form of activity, another form of exercise briefly, then return to the original task. Repeating this strategy encourages the brain to utilize redundant neuro pathways to complete the task. This takes time and patience.

DIFFERENTIATED STIMULUS: As it relates to exercise or physical activity, differentiated stimulus employs a variety of movements, engaging a spectrum of both fine and gross motor skills. This, of course, applies to interventions used in physical/occupational therapy. Rather than forming a set routine, develop a freelance approach that utilizes fine and gross motor movements. Attempt new activities (within safe limits). Take up sketching, play an instrument, build models, learn to knit, and so forth. Remember, the outcome is not the product itself, but the process!

SOCIALIZATION: Physical activity is much more enjoyable when we have others to share it with, and to encourage us along the way. There may be a fitness/wellness center in your local hospital (they can adapt activities for us MSA folks). Find a workout partner who can guide you (and be there in case you need assistance). Maybe there's a watercolor or pottery class in your local community center. You get the idea.

By developing and implementing a personal treatment plan (PTP), we may be able to build and strengthen our abilities - or at least extend the time we have them. We must strive to not rely on walkers and wheelchairs and so forth before we absolutely must have them. Research shows that their continued use creates new neural pathways in the brain, specific to their use, making it more difficult to perform tasks without them.

I hope you'll find these suggestions encouraging. I know we're each at different stages with MSA rot and we have different abilities. Yours in health and hope.

...ever feel like you're in free-fall?

dataMSA.com

February 2, 2016

Happy Tuesday!

All of us have faced that horrible moment when, after months of testing and screening, we receive our diagnosis. Of course, we ask - "What can be done? What is the treatment for MSA?" And we then get another emotional wallop... we hear - "There is no cure, there is no treatment for MSA. There isn't much we can do." We might even hear - "I don't think you'll need to come back here because we can't really help you."

Holy Smoke! Some of us may have been offered a sense of hope in the form of interventions, like physical therapy or meds to reduce symptoms. I tried the PT. The center was not at all familiar with MSA and kept repeating - "Let's just try a little harder." After weeks of doing the same thing over and over again, the insurance ran out. At least I had the sense to ask how I could fall more safely.

Drs. offered meds to reduce my tremors, to stabilize my blood pressure (to prevent falls), to reduce incontinence / encopresis, and so forth. I refused them all (except one: a mild antidepressant. It surely helps when the challenges seem overwhelming).

I was fortunate to be in excellent physical health, so I focused on maintaining and strengthening my cognitive and motor skills. I drew on my experiences as a special-needs teacher. It surely wasn't an easy road and it isn't easy today, but I know this approach has helped me.

"No cure". Okay, I can accept that for now.

"Nothing can be done". That, I refuse to accept.

There are things we can do for ourselves to enrich the quality and length of life. If you haven't had the chance, scan through my previous posts for the last month or so.
Remember, too, the dataMSA Survey for Multiple System Atrophy is still open. This survey collects patient-driven information from patients, caregivers, and loved ones of those lost to MSA. More than 350 folks worldwide have added their experiences.

To view the survey results, click here: www.dataMSA.com

There are things we can do - more later.

Yours in health and hope-

February 4, 2016

This MSA rot is like riding a roller coaster. I've always hated roller coasters. Oh well...

February 5, 2016

In the classroom, I would look for unique, magical 'teachable moments', during which everything seemed spot-on for learning. I did so again today.

Last night, it seemed my tired body was responding to music I couldn't hear. There were twitches and spasms and tremors. And wonky eyes. And labored breathing. An MSA dance party for 1 —

This morning, I was a wreck. Weak as water and utterly useless. I could barely hold my head up...so I quit trying and plopped into the pillows. After a looong snooze, I re-awoke and decided to push back, as I usually do. This time though, it wasn't going well.

Ah, the 'teachable moment'. I took stock of what was what and ran through a variety of small interventions. Something had to work. Walking across the room? Nope. Trying to hold a fork? Nope. What could it be? Maybe, my sense of sight...

I opened my eyes as wide as I could and scanned the room. Dean thought I was going a bit mad, but I kept at it. I looked toward light, toward movement in the trees outside. I kept distracting myself through my vision for several minutes. Then, I tried to do a few things. I repeated the process a few times. Eventually, I was able to hold a mug, a fork, able to swallow, to move about. Nothing earth-shattering yet amazing all the same.

After an hour or so, I went back to bed for more rest. I can report at this hour, I am somewhat back to normal (whatever that is). Before I applied neural-training interventions, a cycle like this would run from 1-3 days. I know all this may sound very simplistic....

Lighter symptoms, shorter duration, less severity. That's my goal. Tomorrow, I'm volunteering at a local school; I sure won't have time for this rot.

Yours in health and hope –

I hope this Monday treated you well...

In the years I've been posting here, I've received a number of questions regarding diagnosis (and about doctors who may not know much about MSA).

I took a look at responses to this question in the dataMSA Survey:

- How many neurologists did the individual consult during the diagnosis process?

While most were seen by at least 2 neurologists, out of 305 responses, 45 had been seen by only one neurologist. A few others had never seen a neurologist. One was diagnosed by a friend, who was a Geriatric Specialist, a few were diagnosed by their GP. One was diagnosed initially by a cardiologist (then sought a neurologist). Another was tested by a neuropsychologist.

This is rather troubling, isn't it? The presenting symptoms can fall under an umbrella of many diseases. While MSA can't be diagnosed with accuracy until necropsy, it is essential to obtain as much data as possible to exclude other diagnoses.... autonomic system testing is very critical.

In 2009, my GP of many years noticed curious symptoms. He referred me to a neurologist who, after much testing, felt strongly that I was suffering from a spinal stenosis. I was then referred to a neurosurgeon who vehemently disagreed. I was then referred to a neurologist who specialized in neurodegenerative disorders. After a battery of exams, he suspected MSA, but would not go further until another neurologist confirmed his results. Eventually, I received a thorough run-through at Mayo Clinic, and a records review at Miami Jackson.

My experiences have taught me this:
- Don't accept the first diagnosis, regardless of who provides it. Keep searching for answers. If you don't have many resources in your community, ask your doctors to send your records to a recognized neuro-center for review.
- Don't live the diagnosis. Fight back as much as you can to retain the skills and abilities you have. It can be quite hard, but essential
for extended quality of life.
- Recognize that no one knows everything about this family of neurodegenerative disorders. Seek information and strategies - but beware of becoming overwhelmed by it all. You must retain a sense of self-empowerment to push back in all ways possible.

Wellness is not only the state of the brain and body, it's also the state of the mind. Keep at it...

February 15, 2017

The ocean is my sanctuary. I come to heal my body and soul. I come to fight physical and emotion changes. I come to recharge and reset. It helps to have the ocean as a neighbor. We've been friends for years.

February 20, 2016

Fought hard this morning...yesterday and last night were pretty darned difficult. I felt weak as water this morning (with that dreaded MSA exhaustion), but I knew if I didn't try to fight it, I'd be in bed all day. I applied neuro training techniques and slowly began to get myself going. Eventually I was able to get here.

The smile represents victory, but I'm still in a funk...a bit depressed. Oh well... onward I go. The goal is to walk a 1/2 mile.

Mar 8, 2016

Fear can be a powerful motivator. When I have a day like yesterday, I lie in bed for hours and I worry about what lies ahead. Nightmares cause me to scream aloud. But when, like a stormfront, it passes, I take stock of myself, my strengths . . . and then I push to get going again.

March 9, 2016

The very day I was told I likely had this neuro rot...and that my life was going to change in many ways, I bought this old Chris Craft cruiser. I named her Eventide because the word reflected calmness and tranquility. She was originally launched in 1970 at the Chris Craft plant where my grandfather worked as a draftsman for many years.

It was a seemingly impractical purchase at the time... with me falling and stumbling about; some friends urged me to sell her. "Too dangerous for you," they said. But I knew what was best for me...not giving up. I still have Eventide; she's a big part of my physical therapy and an even bigger part of my well-being.

March 10, 2016
Folks ask what I've been doing to stay 'afloat'... Well, from the day of diagnosis, I never quit fighting. I stayed active when I could, I kept a clear focus. I set goals; I adjusted and readjusted them often. More importantly, I focused my spirituality. I aligned myself. I found harmony. Peace. Acceptance, but never resignation.

Mar 11, 2016
I pushed against my limits today; I got pretty tired. When I'm really tired, I walk sideways like a crab. That's okay...crab walking is still walking!

Mar 13, 2016
Today, I awoke with that damned MSA rot fatigue. It can be so debilitating, but I know it's not 'real' fatigue... I always try neural training techniques to resist it. They don't always work. Today, they did.

March 15, 2016
I'm fighting to push back the enemy this morning... I've had to retreat to headquarters to reorganize and develop new strategies of attack.

March 20, 2016

Good news - researchers at Mayo Clinic/Rochester, under Dr. Phillip Low, will be analyzing and utilizing the dataMSA Survey databases. Their group is currently preparing a large (physician-driven) query to assess risk factors of MSA on a broad basis – and state that the dataMSA patient-driven data will be a vital complement to this effort.

Dr. Wolfgang Singer, Mayo Clinic Department of Neurology, stated, "I believe efforts like this should be shared with the medical community ... and should be published as a manuscript in a pertinent medical journal."

Thank you, everyone, for making this project such a fine success. I will keep you posted as this collaboration with Mayo Clinic proceeds. I hope you will share this with information your MSA groups and friends.

March 30, 2016

I did it. I pushed myself this afternoon. I hadn't ridden in several months...and I didn't get very far...that's okay. My neural training research suggests that differentiated stimulus (DS) can promote neuroplasticity. Unlike physical therapy (PT), which generally uses a few activities repeated in cycles, DS utilizes a wide variety of fine and gross motor activities to stimulate redundant neuropathways. It's a challenge...but one worth taking!

April 19, 2016

During an appointment a week or so ago, I asked my neurologist if there was any chance I'd been misdiagnosed. After all, in the original MSA prognosis given 60 months back, my Echo

146

Tango Delta was to be sometime this summer...and it's clear I haven't finished packing.

He basically said, "no", as he referred to data collected during my clinical trial a few years back and his own assessments and observations. We then talked about the amazing science of neural training, which I have been employing for a couple of years.

At any rate, it's clear my departure has been delayed awhile. Since there's no sense hanging around at the loading gate, I've started unpacking and putting pieces of my life back where they belong.

ETD on hold. It's just as well - I wasn't quite ready.

April 20, 2016

I feel like I'm cheating death. I've done it before - On April Fool's Day 2005, I suffered an abdominal aneurysm and teetered on the tightrope between this world and the other.

And now I seem to be outpacing the threat of Multiple System Atrophy. But why? Why am I able to carry on when others haven't?

Could it be my age? I was 53 when I was diagnosed. Data indicates the 32% of MSA patients are diagnosed at age 55 or younger, so perhaps age is a minor factor.

Could it be that I was fit and healthy prior to diagnosis? The ability to remain active is essential when facing any illness, but there are others who were in good health prior to MSA, only to be left debilitated and disabled.

Could it be about attitude? I have approached MSA as I would any obstacle, with tenacity and strategic planning to overcome it. I employ neural training, exercise, meditation and diet

147

to better my odds. But many others have done these things, experiencing far less successful outcomes.

Perhaps it's faith - faith in a spiritual alignment that will guide me toward my potential. Well, no doubt this helps emotionally. But can we then assume that others who are more severely affected by MSA have less faith than I? Of course not. Many stoic individuals of great faith and spiritual strength have succumbed to MSA.

So why am I staying out in front of this rot? It's likely I'll never know the answer. So, I'll just carry on with gratitude- and wonder.

April 26, 2016

My eyes are wicked sensitive and heavy, my breathing is shallow, I feel chilled and weak. What's that time, kids? MSA symptom cycle!

April 27, 2016

I get totally taken down with MSA rot about once every 7-10 days. This rate has been holding pretty steady for the past year. However, the severity and duration I experience are much less since I've been applying neural training strategies.

May 4, 2016

MSA had affected my ability to perspire...by the time I did, it was often too late, and I was in danger. An ability to sweat is critical here in south Florida. Using neural training/differentiated stimuli, I retrained my brain to initiate sweating much earlier; it took about a year. Today, I was drenched...and I was elated!

Many of us heard that there was nothing that could be done for MSA- there was no cure, there was no treatment. When I heard this, I didn't quite believe it and decided to fight. I started researching interventions for individuals with traumatic brain injury.

Having worked in special education for a number of years, I questioned if strategies for traumatic brain injury could be effective for organic brain injury.

Neural training is not easy. The results don't come quickly, and the interventions require a great deal of patience. For me, the investment has paid dividends.

Not a cure, but certainly a viable treatment and a course toward improving quality of life.

Some days are quite hard.

dataMSA.com

May 11, 2016

I think most of you know I write children's books...and, when I can, I enjoy going to schools to meet with students of all ages. This time of year, I keep pretty busy- I try to make it to a couple of schools a week. It wears me out, but it gives my days meaning. I'm grateful that I can do it!

May 16, 2016

Today, I got up, got dressed, and got out- but I didn't get far before I got back in, got undressed and got back into bed. I'll try again tomorrow!

May 25, 2016

Well, gang - I learned a lesson the hard way (and the painful way). Because MSA presents such a wide and varied menu of symptoms, and because those symptoms are always changing and shifting, I failed to mention some 'experiences' I was going through to my primary doctor.

Turns out, for many, many months, I've been having a very severe reaction to Lovastatin. I was prescribed Lovastatin because my cholesterol numbers were high/average. Because MSA has rendered me more sedentary, my dr wanted to ensure that those numbers didn't climb.

While I was sorting out dealing with daily/weekly/monthly MSA rot, I began to experience strong pain in my jaw. I wrote it off to muscle spasms at night. The pain grew and grew to the point of not being able to open my mouth fully. I talked to my dentist about getting a bite guard. He screened me for TMJ, as well. I think we all have a bit of it...

150

Then, I experienced incidents of brief amnesia, during which I was unable to recall basic facts about my life - my address, my middle name, names of family members. Not even my dog's name. Each episode lasted 4-6 hours. I wrote this off to the memory deficits some MSA patients report.

I soon began to notice that my upper arms seemed to be atrophying. There was no muscle tone at all, and they seemed thin and weaker. I experienced pain in both upper arms, which steadily worsened. My sleep became disrupted by the pain. Again, I assumed it was related to MSA spasms that might have been occurring during sleep.

Recently, in the deep of night, my right arm would seem to be paralyzed. I had to use my left arm to move the right arm while in bed. I was afraid that MSA was gaining ground at a rather rapid pace.

Then, a friend of mine asked if I was taking statin drugs. He mentioned that all of this sounded like severe side effects that a small percentage of statin users experience. I began to do a bit of research. Turns out, in about 2% of users, statin begins to attack systems in the body... it can affect vision, insulin production, respiration and muscle. Some folks actually develop diabetes as a result.

Yesterday, I visited my dr, who immediately pulled the meds. He asked why I had not mentioned any of this to him - and I sheepishly explained that I assumed it was all MSA-related. He replied that regardless of my assumption about a cause, all symptoms should be discussed. I had put myself in danger.

I learned there can be long-term and sometimes irreversible damage to a person who ignores the side effects of statins. It will take at least 7-10 days after stopping the drug for the pain to abate, then I must start the process of rebuilding muscle in my arms, shoulders and neck.

Good grief. The lesson? Always tell your drs about ALL of your symptoms. Don't assume that MSA is the cause of every sign of trouble. If I had spoken up, I could have saved myself this painful and perhaps very harmful situation. By the way, I will be reporting these effects (and my MSA status) to the researchers at the NIH.

Take care of yourself.

May 26, 2016

It's going to take a while longer for the rotten effects of Lovastatin to dissipate. I learned from a friend who was on the board of local Alzheimer's foundation that they were advised to NEVER place an Alzheimer's Disease patient on any statin drug. The effects could be severe.

And recent research indicates that statins, once thought to help prevent/reduce Parkinson's Disease, may actually accelerate the disease and increase Parkinson's symptoms.

Here's a bit from research led by Xuemei Huang, professor of neurology and vice chair for research at Penn State College of Medicine:

- "Statins reduce a compound called coenzyme Q10, which should be investigated for Parkinson's associations in future studies. The compound produces energy for cells and is believed to have protective qualities in nerve cells.

- "Statins have been very important for preventing and treating vascular disease, but we need more research to

152

understand if in some cases there is collateral damage," Huang adds.

He advises that until more research can further interpret the associations between Parkinson's, cholesterol and statins, scientists should remain cautious of promoting the benefits of statins for patients with Parkinson's disease.

I'm upset that while I've been working so hard against MSA, I've been facing debilitating effect of statins - but at least I'm glad to know what I'm up against.

Remember the lesson: always tell you doctor about any and all changes you are experiencing. Never just 'write-off' symptoms to MSA (like I did).

One aspect of MSA that is seldom discussed is the often-crippling financial impact the disease has on individuals and families. Results from the dataMSA Surveys indicate that

- 58.4% of MSA patients were diagnosed prior to age 60, affecting their income potential, their retirement, social security payments and their ability to meet financial needs of their family (college, care for aging parents, etc.)

- 67% of MSA patients were either the sole source of income or a significant contributor to their family's income

-14.3% of MSA patients report that disability income is their only source of income (in the US, government/social security disability income represents approximately 1/3 of the individual's pre-disability income)

- 53.1% of MSA patients lack financial resources needed for adequate care to live comfortably

- 30.8% of MSA patients suffer severe financial hardship

- 12.5% of MSA patients report cannot meet basic life necessities due to financial hardship

- 15.4% of MSA patients cannot acquire health care-related services due to financial hardship.

We often read of our MSA colleagues seeking alternative or experimental treatment, but for those who cannot meet their basic needs due to financial restrictions, this is a 'pipe dream'.

As we seek effective treatments and pathways toward a cure, let us always remember those who face not only the challenges of MSA, but also great financial strain. Their voices are seldom heard in our dialogue.

Perhaps, we can find a way to generate funding to assist our MSA friends who are in dire need today, while we seek funding for those who may be affected tomorrow. Thanks for reading...

June 7, 2016

Yesterday, I wrote about the devastating effects MSA can have on an individual's financial situation. I believe many of us are in the same boat.

While I was undergoing diagnostic procedures 6 years ago, I had to take a medical leave from my teaching position. The leave was unpaid, although I still received health insurance benefits. I expected to return to work; I was only 53 and needed to keep going another 10 years to secure myself financially.

As the diagnosis of MSA was ascertained, I remained on leave until I had no choice but to resign from my job. At that point, I had to pay for COBRA benefits, $700/month - with no income. Luckily, Dean was working, and we managed to get by with my savings and his income. We gave up our home and found a 600square foot rental. We cut out most of our discretionary spending.

I sought Social Security Disability, which took some time. I eventually began receiving disability payments that represented less than 30% +/- of my salary. Remember, that would be 30% of a teacher's salary. Of course, I had to wait 2 years to qualify for Medicare insurance...so I kept paying $700/mo. However, this insurance did not cover a home health aide, so while Dean was working, I had to manage alone... for the past 6 years. Sometimes, his work took him out of town. I was always grateful for the kindness of friends.

How lucky we were when a good friend stepped in to assist us. With her help, we recently arranged for Dean to retire at 62. His being home allows me to take better care of myself, to push against my perceived limits, to feel safe from a fall and injury while being alone (which was happening often).

When I created dataMSA, I did so to allow us patients and our caregivers to express what MSA looks like day by day from our perspective. I wanted other patients to know what was 'normal', to bring a bit of clarity to an overwhelming mystery. I wanted to give us a collective voice that could ring loudly to researchers and medical providers.

This summer, Mayo Clinic will be using the dataMSA Survey results to identify trends, which may lead to new research for treatment and/or a cure. But how might we in the MSA community better use this same data to help one another, to seek resources, to improve the quality of life for our colleagues?

The effects of MSA are devastating. We all know that far too well. Those stricken shouldn't have to suffer from poverty, as well. I welcome your ideas.

Thanks for reading.

Jul 1, 2016

"Pride goeth before a fall." Well, not so much pride, and I didn't literally fall. But, after enjoying some fine days, I'm experiencing the worst night and morning I've had in months. Damned rot.

July 23, 2016

I feel changes...emotional and cognitive. At times, I feel swamped, overwhelmed. So, I come to the ocean whenever I can - as I have done since I was a child...my place of healing and restoration.

July 28, 2016

With a post reach of 2-3K weekly, I get asked a lot of questions; the most common one is, "Do you have any advice for someone newly diagnosed with MSA?" Here's my reply in a nutshell:

1) If at all possible, secure a 2nd or 3rd opinion (hopefully from specialists familiar with MSA). This is a challenging (nearly impossible) disease to diagnose accurately and other illnesses may present very similar symptoms.

2) Fight back immediately. Stay physically active. If you're not active now, become active. Engage in exercises that will employ a variety of fine and gross motor skills. I have found typical physical therapy to be ineffective...read up on interventions for persons with brain injury to get a better understanding of what may work for you. I used to work with children who suffered traumatic brain injury...I began to question if the brain knows the difference between traumatic and organic damage. Apparently, it doesn't. So, access the research!

3) Don't utilize support devices until they are really necessary. Some of us use canes and walkers to assist with mobility...some use them to aid balance. But be careful. Relying on devices too early on may result in the brain/body adjusting to

dependency on them. Do what you must to stay safe yet challenge yourself to maintain the skills you have.

4) Stay socially active. Some of us feel like we want to stay secluded because our symptoms may seem embarrassing. Perhaps it just seems easier to pop on the TV and relax. However, it's a bad course of action. Socialization (in person, not through social media) requires the brain to utilize many functions: interpreting social cues, engaging conversational speech, auditory discrimination and so forth. While one-on-one is good, 2 or 3 folks is better. Challenge yourself. A little self-conscious? Explain to the group that you may need things repeated once in a while...

5) MSA presents fatigue. It's debilitating. But it's not real. I was told, early on, that these long episodes could be the result of my brain seeking new neuropathways. Perhaps these signs of fatigue were good. But the episodes started to come more frequently, and the duration grew longer. Eventually, I found myself stuck in bed for up to 72 hours at a time. My fear was that the episodes would close in on each other and I would be bedridden, or wheelchair bound. I decided to fight back. On my webpage- www.dataMSA.com , there is information on the neurotraining techniques I have employed for the past 18+ months with good results. In the early stages, you may allow yourself some down time, but don't surrender to fatigue

6) Use meds as sparingly as possible. In the early stages, I declined all meds for blood pressure, tremors, spasms, sleep disorder, etc. I wanted to know what I was up against so I could try to fight back. Both our motor and autonomic neuropathways have redundant or parallel pathways available. Ever hear that we

use only 60% of our brain? That other 40% isn't sitting off to one side, dormant. It's comprised of un-utilized or under-utilized pathways. Through neurotraining (as discussed above), there is potential to engage those pathways to compensate for damaged pathways.

7) There's a lot written about diet... I can't begin to summarize it all here. After reading and attempting to follow a few prescribed diets, I decided to exercise moderation. I cut out all artificial sweeteners and I limit intake of sugar. Moderate fats (don't cut them out), don't skimp on protein. I try to avoid all artificial ingredients (tough one) and all processed food. A balanced diet of fresh and natural foods takes away a lot of the worry. If you smoke or drink heavily, stop (alcohol and damaged/exposed nerve cells make for a bad combination).

8) Don't allow yourself to become defined by MSA. Read enough, but not too much. Seek support when you need it, but don't become immersed in the discussions. Stay aware of changes to your body and mind as they come and work to push against them. When you reach a point, adjust as needed. It's a tight line we walk as we balance pushing against progression while making adaptations that may be required.

9) I've heard over and over that there's little to nothing that can be done for folks with MSA. Wrong. Totally wrong. As with any disease, the sooner the intervention, the better the results. Cure? No, not yet. But you can improve and extend quality of life by taking specific steps to push back against progression. I'm now 6 years in and I'm realistic. I sense that some things are changing. However, I feel I have a small modicum of control...and that helps me tremendously. At this point, I have far exceeded my prognosis.

I hope this may help. I'm not a specialist, not a doctor, just a guy living day by day with MSA. Be sure to visit my webpage. There, you will find survey responses from more than 450 folks worldwide who are affected by MSA.

August 12, 2016

Well, well, well - despite my best efforts to stay active, I've not been active enough! The 'Phantom Pain' that's been cohabitating my body lately has come from muscle atrophy (very common in MSA)! Muscle atrophy leads to pain; Pain leads to lack of sleep; Lack of sleep leads to inactivity; Inactivity leads to muscle atrophy. Hmmm. I have to push back harder when I'm able to.

August 16, 2016

Folks often ask me what meds/supplements I take. Early on, I was offered meds for tremors, blood pressure, sleep and so forth. I turned them all down. I did try some supplements, but after a proper trial period without significant outcomes, I stopped. Instead, I focused on physical and mental activity through neuro-training, and a balanced, moderate diet with good quality vitamins and probiotics. I was healthy and fit prior to diagnosis and I fight daily to stay that way. Some days, I lose those fights...but I stay focused on the battle plan.

August 20, 2016

It's 1 a.m. and sleep seems a very vague possibility...again. I thought I'd share something I haven't really discussed in the years I've had this FB page- our finances. I was 'officially' diagnosed in July 2010 at the age of 53 in my 22nd year of teaching. However, as with most of us, symptoms were present long before that. Mine led me to cut my employment with the school district to part time. Something was going wrong, but I didn't know what. I was then earning about 60% of my salary.

At about the same time, we were reeling from the fall in the US economy. I had invested in a few small properties for my eventual retirement. Quickly, they were worth next to nothing. By the time my diagnosis was clarified that summer, I was on unpaid leave from the school district. Although my health insurance was still covered, I had no income. SSDI was applied for and approved rather quickly, for which I was grateful. But I received only about 32% of my salary and had to pay $750/month for COBRA health coverage when my leave expired.

Dean and I scrambled to adjust to our new lives. All the investment properties had to go back to the bank; we lost everything we had in them. We rented a 630 square-foot house and prepared for the outcome of my dire diagnosis... 66-72 months life expectancy.

A very kind woman who has looked out for me for the past 35+ years (just after the suicide of my father) stepped in to help cover the care of my health insurance for the 2 years before Medicare eligibility. I'm not sure what we would have done otherwise.

We carried on with only Dean's salary and my SSDI until Fall 2015 when it became increasingly apparent I needed a home health aide while Dean was at work or travelling for work (sometimes for 2-3 weeks at a time). On my very bad days, I would lie in bed alone with our dog, unable to do much of anything for myself. I was at risk each time I tried to reach the bathroom. Sadly, my Medicare plan would only pay for a few days of home care per month.

Dean was 61 at the time. After much discussion, we took the plunge and decided that he should retire early so I could put up a stronger fight against MSA. Of course, this meant he would have no salary for 10 months until he was eligible for Social Security. His first check is due to arrive late next month.

By now, our savings are pretty well depleted. We both have 401Ks from which we can draw moderately. Neither of us had high-paying jobs. There were no contributions to my retirement account in the past 6 years; I had expected to contribute for another 10 years when I had to resign my job. Teachers may make a difference, but they don't make much money.

Yet, how lucky we are. We have each other. Dean's health is good and, aside from MSA, so is mine. We have no children to see through school, we have no ailing family to care for, so we'll get by...

Nearly 50% of the participants in the dataMSA Annual Update Survey report that MSA has created severe financial hardship for the patient/family.

14% report having to sacrifice basic life necessities because of hardship, such as mortgage payment, clothing, etc.

17% report being unable to acquire health care/support services due to hardship.

21% report having needed services/support denied by their health insurance carrier.

56% report living at a great distance from medical care/support

We are all hopeful for effective treatments...supplements, therapies, programs and so forth. But many in our MSA community are facing severe hardship, something we must keep in mind. They may never be able to access the services that could improve their quality of life.

I wish I had a solution. Thanks for reading

August 22, 2016

I've been going to my GP, Dr. Stinson, for nearly 20 years (not long after he opened his practice). I had selected his name from a list of local providers who were covered by School Board insurance. It really mattered little to me... I never went to the doctor anyway and I never needed to.

A bit more than 6 years ago, during an annual check-up (I usually skipped them, but an aortic bleed quickly put me in line), he asked about observations he had made: "Why do you favor your left leg? How long have your hands tremored?" I replied that it was likely due to a sprained muscle or the unpleasant signs of hitting 50+. He didn't agree.

His series of tests landed me in a neurologist's office. Then, came more tests, which were confirmed by even more tests and records reviews from Mayo Clinic and Miami Jackson.

"What is it?" I'd ask Dr. Stinson.

He'd reply, "Let's wait and see."

Finally- a diagnosis: Multiple System Atrophy. "I suspected this," Dr. Stinson explained in our consultation.

"But how? It's so rare. No one seems to know much about it."

"Because my father has it, he replied. "He was diagnosed about 6 years ago."

How fortunate I've been to be under the care of a doctor who knows the disease so well. As a D.O., he has supported me in my approach to avoid medications. He monitors my levels for deficiencies and guides through holistic approaches. We focus on exercise and diet. I share with him my successes with neural training.

As my symptoms approach and/or advance, he relates them to his father's experiences and the many accommodations he made at various stages of his MSA journey. His words bring me great comfort.

I'm also lucky to have a very fine neurologist, who cared for Dr. Stinson's father and is well acquainted with MSA. But nothing calms me more than a nice conversation with Dr. Stinson.

Dr. Stinson's father died a couple of years ago. He was in his late 70's. We talk about his father, his path, his struggle, his eventual death. Neither of us shy away from it, nor do we dwell on it. It just is.

I found an MSA mentor in my long-trusted doctor... and a trusted friend. In spite of all the MSA mysteries in the universe, these stars have aligned for me.

August 27, 2016

I'm determined to fight this goddamned muscle atrophy! The myalgia hurts like hell...but it isn't going to consume me. Monday, I start physical therapy (whatever my insurance will cover). I'm hoping for some massage therapy, too. Meanwhile, I am using hand weights and doing stretching/relaxation exercises.

August 30, 2016

In a painful PT session this morning, I learned I've been pushing myself a bit too hard! By not recognizing some mobility/movement limits, brought about by MSA, I've injured my shoulders. It may take weeks to heal this. So, fight back, but be safe. Seek guidance.

August 31, 2016

A fine morning after a challenging night....

As you may have read yesterday, I must undergo several sessions of PT to repair damage I did to my shoulders. Was it MSA related? Perhaps. Was it related to pushing 60? Likely. Was it related to being stubborn and headstrong? Yes, most certainly.

I want to clarify my thoughts about PT. When I was diagnosed at 53, I was fit and in good shape. Not an athlete, but active. When I was told there was little that could be done, I balked.

Through my years working with special needs children, especially those with TBI (traumatic brain injury), I understood that neural training needed to be my primary strategy. Neural training utilizes the plasticity of the brain to recover skills lost/impaired through injury (whether organic or traumatic).

A child who experiences a TBI stands a greater chance of recovery than an adult in a similar situation (dependent, of course, on location/severity of the injury).Therefore, it is essential to assess the individual's situation when prescribing any PTP (personal treatment plan) by taking into account age, premorbid abilities, current abilities, and -in our cases - expected/observed rate of progression or degeneration.

165

My research led me to accept that PT/OT was unlikely to promote high levels of success I was seeking in my neural-training plan. Because I was active and strong, I needed activities that would stimulate/develop the redundant neuropathways needed toward skill retention/recovery.

This is not to say PT/OT have no use for us MSA folk. Movement therapy, strength building, balance, daily living skills are all essential (and, in hindsight, a bit of PT might have guided me to plan safer interventions for myself!). But those with higher levels of physical ability may want more- (visit www.dataMSA.com to learn about my journey with neural training).

My advice for everyone -regardless of age, condition, diagnosis, prognosis, hocus-pocus - is to find activity that fits you. Do something physical every day to the very best of your abilities ...be determined to keep going in any way you're able. Set the bar just high enough to challenge yourself...and never compare yourself to others. It's your plan, your journey.

Oh, and remember to keep safety in mind. I'm headed back to PT tomorrow to heal these injured shoulders.

Carry on!

September 7, 2016

Some may doubt me...heck, sometimes I doubt myself, but I think this neuro- training is still working. Not only can I now walk a quarter mile in the sand, I have started running again. It's been very gradual, but I can feel the skill coming back. No, I can't do this every day. In fact, there are still days I can barely get out of bed...but there is definite improvement!

I've been exploring and implementing neuro training techniques for more than 2 years now. If you'd like to learn more, visit my web page: www.dataMSA.com. Thank you always for your interest and support.

September 8, 2016

In the past two and a half years, I've read every one of the 450+ responses to the dataMSA surveys. Every word. As an MSA patient myself, I find the information informative- but often haunting.

Last night was challenging. It felt as if all sequencing of my cognition had been disconnected. Very uncomfortable. I'm exhausted this morning.

On a strong day, I get about 4 hours during the day where I can tend to my errands, my chores. My volunteer work, my exercise. Then, I must rest for a few hours and, if I govern myself, I can have a pleasant evening.

Then there are the days when I lose myself in system failures. I must push myself to hold my head up, to keep my eyes open, to breath. Even on these days, I set goals. Small goals.

Each day with MSA is like a walk in dense woods...at once awe-inspiring, overwhelming, intimidating.

September 9, 2016

Yesterday was a 'lost day'...I was bedridden and exhausted. Despite trying to jump start myself, I had no luck and had to miss a physical therapy for my shoulders.

Today, despite being sore, I'm up and about. Perhaps, being aboard Eventide is the best therapy of all!

September 20, 2016

"Eureka!" as Archimedes would say, I've discovered a formula related to MSA! $a=2(r)$, wherein "a" represents activity and "r" represents rest. Simply stated, with relation to MSA, every unit of activity will require twice its value in rest.

What's that? You already knew this? So, it's no "eureka" discovery? Well, onto the next experiment!

September 24, 2016

I don't think what I'm going through tonight is MSA...it's CTE-related. Terrible. Brain shorting. Hurts. Tired of it.

October 19, 2016

Last night, I had a Parkinsonian Extravaganza....and it wasn't at all fun. It started with a rash of obsessive thoughts I could not settle. That was accompanied by restlessness in my limbs, which soon developed into tremors and rocking. Before long, I had muscle spasms. No matter how I tried, I could not still my arms, hands, and legs from jerking and flopping about.

This went on for a few hours. Of course, sleep was out of the question. I tried to implement some of the neural training techniques I've been using, but they failed to have any affect.

Eventually, perhaps from exhaustion, I fell asleep for a couple of hours. When I awoke, there was no trace of the episode and, aside from being tired, I am fully functional this morning.

Just an FYI- I am diagnosed MSA-P. I've experienced many Parkinson's symptoms in the past, but nothing quite like this in severity or duration.

November 7, 2016

Folks who live with MSA (or any disease in the same family of illnesses) see continual, incremental changes in their abilities. Over a period of time, we adapt and adjust to our 'new' selves.

For the past few years, as many of you know, I've been implementing a strategy of neural training, similar to that used for TBI (traumatic brain injury). To know with any certainty if I'm doing anything effective, I return to the baseline data collected early into my disease. From there, I can determine areas in which MSA is progressing and areas in which I may be slowing advancement.

From this information, I develop (and modify as needed) a treatment plan that prioritizes areas of greatest concern. For example, I've recently learned that my arms are starting to fail; my left arm in particular has lost much of its strength. Because a prior attempt at strength training on my own resulted in injury, it's time to turn to a specialty gym/wellness center for help.

As long as I'm able to push against the progression of MSA, I plan to continue this strategy... it appears to have (+) outcomes. Of course, there are still signs of degeneration, but I triage specific issues and approach them head-on.

For some perspective, I was 53 at diagnosis (MSA-P) and was above average in fitness. I was a cyclist and a bit of runner. During early stages, I made a point of trying to retain and strengthen my fine and gross motor skills. As a teacher of youth with special needs, I had seen the (+) effects of neural training in TBI and wondered if organic brain injury would respond similarly.

Not a cure...just an experiment. Maybe it can help you in your journey...

November 9, 2016

Gee, this morning I learned that both my arms have atrophied a great deal. I've lost 70% use of my left arm. I knew it was bad, but I didn't know it was that bad. I was told, given the rate of deterioration, I am on track to lose grip and dexterity in my left hand before too long.

I say, Hell no! I'm developing and will implement a treatment plan, as I did when my legs were starting to fail. This will involve specific interventions guided by a trainer at our hospital fitness center.

November 19, 2016

I've been approaching my visits to the gym the way I approach all my interventions, through the lens of neural-training. Aside from the goal of recovering lost strength due to atrophy, I'm attempting to trigger new neuropathways through movement stimulation. I also employ differentiated stimulus techniques. Science based, but experimental. More on that a bit later.

Trouble is, I have a set amount of energy - similar perhaps to a cell phone with a weak battery. If I use the energy in physical training, there is little left for daily activity.

A nap helps but doesn't really recharge me...and if I experience insomnia at night, the plan is shot for a while. None the less, I am going to keep at it. It surely isn't easy (at times, depressing), but I see no alternative. I must fight to retain the skills I have and try to restore some I've lost.

November 21, 2016

I pushed too hard physically and socially and I am paying for it. My nerves are on edge, I'm in a cloud of depression... there's a scream in me trying to get out. I know I have to keep fighting this rot, day by day-I'm afraid I'll lose ground quickly if I don't.

I get so tired. It's not all sunshine and roses, is it? But, oh how lucky I am for the strength I have. So... no more complaints.

November 29, 2016

Last night wasn't so good... my blood pressure went wonky and I wound up on the floor, doing a close-up inspection of the woodwork (it needs touch up). I don't remember much about it, really. I must have clunked my head when I landed... I'm rather sore this morning. Luckily, Dean and Lady the Wonderdog found me and got me to bed safely. Sometimes, this damned rot catches you completely off guard.

December 1, 2016

After 2 years, has neuro-training had any notable (+) effect? I am certain it has. After this Holiday season passes, I'll begin to aggregate data I've collected, pre and post implementation. My informal observations indicate that some skills have improved, others have not...drs. note the progression has slowed. Stay tuned!

December 2, 2016

I've been implementing neural-training techniques at the gym. At this point, I'm far more interested in stimulating new neuropathways than in building endurance or strength. My goal with neural training is to bypass damaged pathways by engaging redundant/parallel pathways, employing strategies utilized for victims of traumatic brain injury.

Interestingly, while my gross motor skills may be seeing improvement, my fine motor skills/tremors may have worsened a bit. Nonetheless, I'll keep at it.

In my 'Not-So-Scientific Clinical Trial for 1", the objectives are:

a) to determine if neural training may be a viable intervention to retain/strengthen neuro-motor functions and corresponding autonomic activity,

b) to determine if neural training may effectively slow/retard MSA progression.

Or, perhaps, the objective is:

c) to take the lead in A Race Against Time! Stay tuned.

December 25, 2016

The rot got me this Christmas morning, but I'll bounce back before you can say 'Good King Wenceslas'! Ho ho ho...

December 30, 2016

For a month, I've been implementing neural-training strategies in my workout sessions... Is it working? I think so. It may be helping retain, perhaps recover some abilities in my arms. My core is stronger, my balance has improved.

Of course, I still experience days lost to this MSA rot. And when I'm bedbound, I dream of going at it again.

2017

Jan 4, 2017

What a difference a day can make. This morning I was strong enough to get to the gym...the trainer stated that I have made good progress compared to my baseline data one month ago. As you know, I have been implementing neuro-training techniques - and I'll keep at it!

Jan 16, 2017

My nighttime MSA jaw clenching caused me to fracture a tooth. Then, MSA-rot made today's procedure for a crown nearly unbearable. Tremors, choking... I'm beat.

the wind will blow.

hang on.

February 5, 2017

All last week, I struggled to get sleep...and exhaustion was starting to lay claim on me.

When my sleep cycle goes far awry, I use edible cannabis (pot brownies) at night to re-set. It takes a few nights, but eventually, I can get REM sleep again. I only use these edibles when I need to.

We can't fight against MSA symptoms if we are not well rested...and I am determined to keep fighting!

February 13, 2017

I fight back against MSA progression and symptoms each day that I can by implementing neurotraining/brain plasticity strategies. But nights remain extremely challenging. I bolt awake with an 'explosion' in my wee brain followed by a symphony of neuro-shorts, flashes of light, patterns and colors. I feel chilled and overheated at the same time. My arms and legs spasm. I try to sit on my hands to squelch the involuntary movement...to no avail.

I have an impulse to run, so I walk the house slowly (falls are a risk). It's a very uncomfortable experience on the whole. Eventually I find respite in a spare room where the television drones me back into a state of calmness.

Ingesting cannabis (brownies) helps extend my sleep to prevent exhaustion, but it doesn't combat these shorting-out experiences. I celebrate a night of decent sleep because it doesn't happen often.

Throughout the term of my illness, I have tried many over-the counter and holistic supplements...none worked and each produced undesirable side effects.

176

This morning, after a rotten night, I wanted to crawl under the covers and hibernate. Instead, I pushed back and went to the wellness center...which didn't go well. But how lucky I am, in spite of this, to be doing this well 6.5 years in to my MSA experience!

February 18, 2017

I've been having a rough go of it these recent days. Thursday morning, I had an emotional drs. visit. That night, we thought Lady the Wonderdog was facing her end of days. Her respiration and heart rate were unstable. This continued into Friday, which resulted in near total decompensation for me.

Today, both Lady and I are resting ...and Dean and I are hopeful that Lady will be with us a bit longer.

April 6, 2017

I just never know which brain I'm going to be working with... Will it be the befuddled brain that can't recall the names of friends, of streets, of nearby towns? The one that becomes overwhelmed and confused easily over simple things?

Or will it be the cross-wired brain, which cannot process normal levels of stimulation? Ordinary light and sound become amplified to uncomfortable levels, causing me to bury my head under pillows while I wait it out.

Or the nervous brain that produces hyper responses to day to day situations through impulsivity and inappropriate emotional behavior? Crying, withdrawal or anger are quick to present.

Or, the empty brain, a dark place, where short/intermediate term memory is absent? The effort to recall or recapture events spins in a vacuum, an abyss of sorts. The information is there, somewhere. Hidden.

Or, the fearful brain, which is awash in hopelessness and despair? The future is bleak, the reality of MSA threatens any sense of peace and balance. Nothing good seems possible.

Or the fragile brain that appears to be functioning fine...until it is over-taxed? At that point, tremors, spasms, twitches and other behaviors present. Fine/gross motor skills decompensate. Even eyelids fail to function properly. Breathing is labored and exhaustion washes over like a tsunami.

And then, there is the normal brain, which allows me to live as if nothing were wrong at all...the one that is allowing me to type this now.

Life with MSA is like a box of chocolates.... you never know what you're gonna get. I'm just grateful to keep gettin'!

May 8, 2017

After our move, I forgot to re-up my Medical Guardian alert system. Well, a hard fall this morning served as an uncomfortable reminder! I was alone when it happened; I'm okay, just sore all over....

May 19, 2017

Yesterday, I spent hour upon hour here (about 30 all told). I tried to force myself up but couldn't. Today, I spent an hour here, up and at 'em. A much better place to be physically... and emotionally.

May 26, 2017

Today, I got up and out for breakfast at a local cafe. I was doing pretty good, until my working tremors started to take over. Soon, I was nearly unable to keep any food on my fork...it landed on the table, my lap, the floor. On top of that, I was having trouble swallowing.

I noticed folks around me watching me, as I tried to steady one hand with the other. My first reaction was embarrassment...then, I thought of explaining my issues. Instead, I just kept at it.

I guess I could have used it as a moment to teach about MSA, but for today I wanted to just be plain ol' me...just like everyone else. Keeping at it, no matter what.

May 31, 2017

I'm so thankful to have such a good doctor looking after me. With the cognitive and emotional changes I'm facing, we're discussing whether to increase my Lexapro or add an anti-anxiety medication to help me cope. Tough call, I hate to take meds.

June 3, 2017

Last night I wound up in the hospital to for an endoscopy to clear blockage in esophagus. Because I am usually able to clear these incidents myself, I waited far too long to seek help - which led to great discomfort.

The good news is that the gastroenterologist who was called in was familiar with MSA, having worked with UM Miami/Jackson - Jackson Memorial Hospital. What a stroke of luck.

Although I had a swallow study done a few years back, of course things progress. He's going to perform an esophageal dilation to improve my swallowing and reduce my choking episodes. There was a silver lining in the storm cloud.

June 5, 2017

Sometimes, especially at night, this MSA rot scares the hell out of me. After collecting patient data from more than 500 folks, I have a rather clear picture of the continuum of the disease. (view all the surveys at www.dataMSA.com)

But I buck up and find determination to fight back. I think if NIKE were to do an awareness ad for MSA, the slogan could read, "Just do it...and then do a bit more." If you can take 10 steps, push to take one more.

Each day, I find strength and inspiration from folks on this page and those I see day to day. Many are suffering far more than

I am from a wide variety of illnesses that weaken and threaten them.

That inspiration allows me to combine my spiritual faith with wicked determination to kick MSA in the chops whenever I'm able to!

July 6, 2017

Well gang, today I had an esophageal dilation in hopes of reducing my choking incidents (which are becoming more and more common). Simple process. The dr. also did some sort of stimulation to the muscle set.

My throat is sore, and my voice is hoarse...I haven't tried to eat much yet. Fingers crossed; throat uncrossed!

July 8, 2017

Seven years ago, I received my initial, working MSA diagnosis. I was told then, based on symptoms and rate of progression, I had about six years to go. Shortly thereafter, that prognosis was restated during my Rifampin clinical trial assessments.

But, today, I turned 60. You have no idea how grateful I am to be bettering the odds...and you know I'm going to keep at it!

July 9, 2017

Thanks, everyone, for the birthday cheer!

Today, I was out at breakfast and struck up a conversation with a woman seated at the counter. She was an oncology nurse and had heard of MSA, although she knew little about it. She stated she worked with neuro-nurses and was very eager to share MSA information with them. We exchanged contact info.

We had a lengthy talk and I directed her to the MSA Coalition website and to dataMSA.com - I am hopeful that this brief interaction will help raise awareness...I try to do so each day that I am able. Perhaps, you are doing the same!

July 10, 2017

Today, I had a consultation with a new neurologist (because we moved to this area). After a brief assessment and review of prior assessments (Mayo Clinic, Holy Cross Medical, Rifampin Clinical Trials), he felt I was doing well. In fact, he thought my prognosis was better than previously stated by others.

He stated that, through further research, we may come to view MSA as a spectrum of disorders (similar to the way we now see autism), with a variety of interventions. Hmm. Maybe!
While in his office, we brought dataMSA.com up on his computer and discussed the findings. He was pleased and surprised...and offered ideas for its usage.

All in all, it was a good day. Exhausting, but good.

July 18, 2017 ·

...just another Tired Tuesday,
sort of a Blues Day.
(need to take a Cruise Day...)
If not mine, then whose day?

August 10, 2017

Yesterday, I had the privilege of speaking about MSA to a Rotary Club in Georgia. While my purpose was to raise awareness, I also stressed the importance of remaining as active as possible. Good advice for everyone!

August 13, 2017

If you had the chance to sit with lead neurologists and MSA researchers at the Cleveland Clinic Lou Ruvo Center for Brain Health for a 1-1 conversation, what would you ask?

Looks like I may have the chance to do just that, and I want to be your voice...I want us all to learn!

If you'd like, send me one or two brief questions and I'll gather them up and put together a list. You may reach me here on FB or through dataMSA at datamsa@yahoo.com
Stay tuned!

August 17, 2017

Good morning, I hope. Last night was rather miserable for me...my wee brain shorted out, presenting 'fireworks'.

Oh well, I awoke today to a very kind note from a gent who recently lost his father to MSA. His words inspired and uplifted me. I hope we are always able to do that for one another...

August 18, 2017

Most of you know I employ strategies of brain plasticity and neuro-training to make living with MSA a bit better. Of course, it's a race against progression; as I work to develop new neuropathways, MSA continues its damage. Luckily, I have seen the quality of my life improve through these efforts.

I am very grateful to pioneers in the field of brain research, like Dr. Diamond, who continued her work while facing criticism, cynicism and sexism. Ultimately, she was proven correct: the brain can change. The race continues...

September 13, 2017

Greetings, all! I haven't anything clever or witty to say today...I don't have any cute Snoopy cartoons. We're here trying to put our house back together after Irma. Had to clean up the residue of mucky, septic water in every room....

How did I fare? Not too well. I collapsed yesterday at a friend's doorstep, likely due to the combination of stress and heat.

But meanwhile, I've been in touch with the Lou Ruvo Brain Center in Vegas! I rescheduled my visit for November and am eager to speak to their team on behalf of us all. More later... stay tuned!

September 20, 2017

Might be post-hurricane stress, or the fall I took...but I'm slipping. Gotta get back up and fight back. Tomorrow.

September 21, 2017

Well, this morning, I have good news...and I have good news! Good news #1 - I found the strength to push back against this rot and was able to exercise and do some light yoga. Hooray!

Good news #2 - I will be meeting with Dr. Mari and Dr. Cummings at the Cleveland Clinic Lou Ruvo Center for Brain Health in Las Vegas on November 09, 10, 11...and I'll be carrying your questions with me.

If you had the chance to meet with these doctors, what would you ask them?

There's still plenty of time for you to send me 1 or 2 questions... I may not be able to ask them all, but I'll do my best! You may post them here or send them to sydnor@hotmail.com

Drs. Mari and Cummings will review all the dataMSA Survey Summaries prior to my visit - here I am at my desk, making sure the website is up to snuff.

October 1, 2017

Life is a series of trade-offs and compromises.

I decided to trade the stressful pace of South Florida for a quieter life in St Augustine. And yes - it has reduced my stress.

But I left behind my doctors, with whom I had established a great rapport. My primary care physician for 20+ years was very familiar with MSA because his father suffered from it. My

185

neurologist was also very well versed in MSA and kept current on the latest research.

Here... well, let's just say things are quite different. I was seen by a nurse practitioner who had no idea what MSA is. Worse, she didn't seem very interested.

I did find a neurologist here - one of two in the area. He was familiar with MSA but did no assessments of any kind. He didn't seem interested in my records. Perhaps it's the "there is nothing we can do for you" approach.

At any rate, I traded off one form of stress for another. Was it a worthwhile trade? I don't know yet. I'll try bowling.

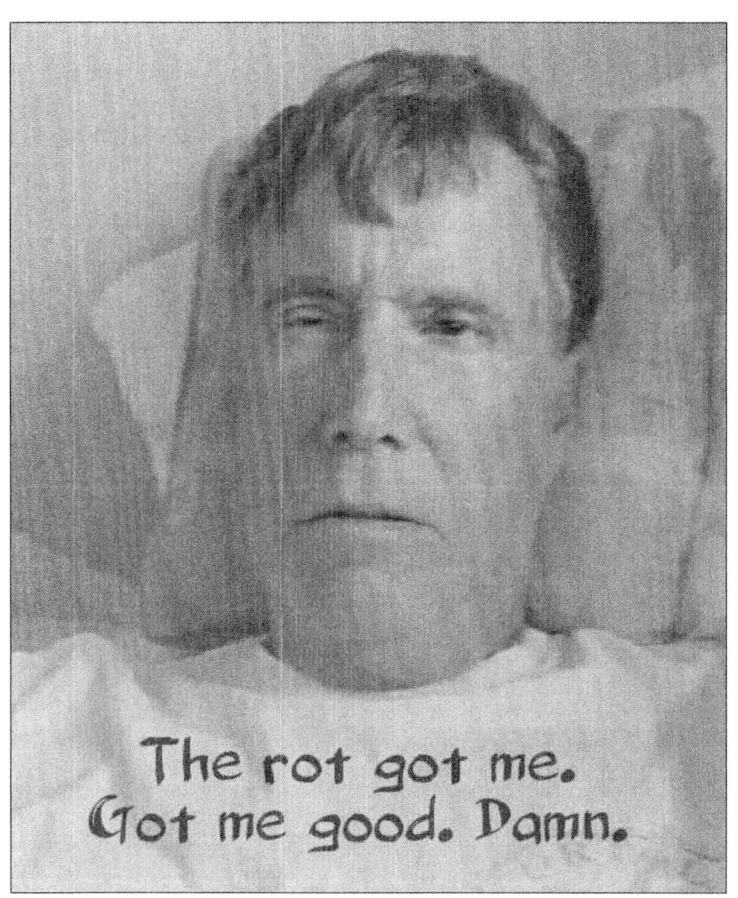

186

October 6, 2017

I was very fortunate to have a 20+ minute telephone conversation this afternoon with Dr. Zoltan Mari at the Cleveland Clinic Lou Ruvo Center for Brain Health in Las Vegas.

He was very interested in the dataMSA Surveys and is eager to put them to use in research for Multiple System Atrophy. We'll be working together to disaggregate and analyze the information for trends, patterns and so forth, with the help of neuro interns.

I thank each of you who shared your experiences.

We also discussed the use of daTscan as a diagnostic tool. The Center considers it the most effective means of pinpointing MSA diagnosis. I'm certain many of us have not had a daTscan and are using other means for diagnosis. Luckily, there are many imaging centers that can provide this test and many insurers cover daTscans. This should be a boost in ensuring proper diagnosis... I'll be getting one ASAP.

I know the daTscan is a controversial topic for many- I will follow up with Dr. Mari this week to obtain more information -

We then discussed the use of Exenatide (Byetta) for treatment of MSA and similar diseases. Byetta, a diabetes drug, is hoped to be an effective treatment to slow progression of MSA by affecting micronuclear neural cells.

Trials for Byetta with regard to Parkinson's have been hopeful - a new FDA Phase 1 Trial will begin in the 1st Quarter of 2018, with hope for prescription by mid-2019. Dr. Mari states this Byetta is currently the greatest hope for treatment of MSA.

Dr. Mari and I will be in contact regularly and I will share all further insights and information I receive...stay tuned! With great hope for better living-

Good day, Everyone! About my previous post regarding daTscan and MSA diagnosis: I have requested information from Dr. Mari (Cleveland Clinic Lou Ruvo Center for Brain Health) that may clarify the current use of daTscans for screening/diagnosis. In the meanwhile, I did a bit of reading (as I know many of you have).

There is a myriad of information regarding daTscan and Parkinson's Disease, but not as much related to MSA. What I did find indicates the following:

a) daTscan is NOT useful for screening/diagnosing MSA-C

b) daTscan CANNOT differentiate between Parkinson's Disease and MSA-P

c) daTscan is NOT 100% effective in diagnosing either PD or MSA-P but is a very useful screening tool, especially in the early stages of symptom presentation

d) daTscan is generally administered when there is question about diagnosis or when symptom presentation is not consistent with diagnosis.

e) daTscan CAN be an accurate and useful tool to differentiate PD from Benign Essential Tremor

Ultimately, my findings indicate that daTscan does NOT confirm nor rule out MSA-P or Parkinson's Disease. In addition, attempts to correlate daTscan results to necropsy findings have been inaccurate at best due to factors affiliated with brain donation (those with rapid progression, those in medical facilities when they died were more likely to donate to the brain banks).

Some of you have asked about the timeline of symptom presentation, diagnosis and death. This limited data is skewed due to the possible inaccuracy of patient reporting and the variances in patients seeking medical attention for symptoms. The rate and severity of symptom progression may accelerate or delay an individual's attempts to seek diagnosis. Additionally, unrelated health issues in each individual, as well as one's age, affect symptom progression and lifespan.

As promised, I will seek clarification on these points from the staff at CCLRCBH. But your posts piqued my curiosity to delve into a bit more! Thanks for helping to keep my mind active

October 9, 2017

As promised, here is Dr. Zoltan Mari's (in photo) response to my inquiry about the use of daTscans in MSA diagnosis- I hope it helps clarify the use of the scan as a diagnostic tool.

"Dear Mr. Sydnor,

I appreciate your question and acknowledge that this situation is a little bit confusing. DaTscan is on label (approved by the FDA) as a confirmatory test for degenerative presynaptic causes of parkinsonism, in case of "indeterminate" Parkinsonism.

In practice, the most common interpretation of the label is such that DaTscan is ordered (and approved/covered by insurance) in cases of tremor, especially with previous history of essential tremor (ET), when Parkinson's disease (PD) is suspected. However, its use can be a lot more inclusive and wider than that very narrow interpretation.

While it is not typically used to confirm MSA specifically, MSA is a form of presynaptic and degenerative form of parkinsonism, when decay of the nigrostriatal system is expected

189

– DaTscan measures the integrity of that system, and thus is expected to be abnormal in DaTscan.

Zoltan Mari, MD

Director, Parkinson's Disease and Movement Disorders Program

Lou Ruvo Center for Brain Health | Las Vegas"

(prior to his position at LRCBH, Dr. Mari was Director, Johns Hopkins Parkinson's & Movement Disorder Center)

Thank you, all, for your questions and comments - they keep me keen to learn more!

November 15, 2017

Howdy, friends. I'm back! Things have been challenging lately. In April, we moved to St Augustine to reduce my stress.

But...Hurricane Irma flooded our new rental home. Now, mold is taking hold and we have to move again...quickly.

This isn't easy at all. More to come. Stay tuned.

December 21, 2017

Despite some challenges in our housing situation lately, I am grateful for all of life's gifts this year. I am thankful to you for your words of encouragement as I journey through MSA... and I am very thankful to those who have shared their MSA experiences on dataMSA.com so others may learn. I wish for each of you a Holiday season of hope, healing and light!

Being alone is not the same as being lonely.

Celebrate your own way.

dataMSA.com

EVEN THO'
YOU'RE
TOSSED
AND WORN,
STEADY ON,
CARRY ON
AS BEST
YOU'RE
ABLE.

2018

January 23, 2018

As many of you know, I am an advocate of increasing physical activity to improve the quality of living with MSA...
but with all the stress of being displaced by hurricane Irma, I was way off track.

Today, I was back at it! I pushed as hard as I dared...and I realized how quickly my skills had deteriorated. To boot, my tremors were worse, swallowing, breathing and other symptoms were elevated. No matter- I'll keep fighting this damned rot. You try, too!

January 24, 2018

This is indeed good news! Below, you can review letters I received from Dr. Mari at the Lou Ruvo Center for Brain Health and his associate at the Henry Ford Hospital regarding use of dataMSA survey results.

Thanks to the nearly 600 of you that shared your MSA experiences so that others may benefit. Sadly, some are no longer with us, but together we can raise their collective MSA voices worldwide.

You may review the dataMSA Survey Summaries at www.dataMSA.com - Wishing the best for us all – BILL

Dear Mr. Sydnor,

Great to hear from you! Happy New Year!

Yes, we have reviewed it and in fact a junior colleague of mine has helped analyze the data – I asked him to email you for permission, but we were planning to submit our abstract to the Movement Society's 2018 meeting. I will check to make sure if he emailed you, we hope this publication will also highlight and bring the right attention to your database.

I am looking forward to working more with the database and do not worry about the DaTscan, it is not a medical urgency. Please keep me posted and always let me know how I can be of help.

Best,

Zoltan Mari, MD

Dear Mr. Sydnor -Good evening.

My name is Abhimanyu Mahajan and I am a neurology resident at Henry Ford Hospital in Detroit. I was introduced to your amazing work (dataMSA.com) by my mentor Dr. Zoltan Mari, who is the Director of movement disorders at the Lou Ruvo Center for Brain Health in Las Vegas.

I must congratulate you on your effort in coming up with such a breadth of information on MSA patients using an online survey. It is truly remarkable and deserves a wider audience. We wish to present your work at the Movement Disorders Society meeting this year. To that effect, we wanted to get your permission for doing so.

Please let us know if that would be OK. If you have any questions, I would be glad to answer them.

Best regards

Abhimanyu

March 28, 2018 ·

I'm tired tonight. So very tired.

The kind of tired that comes from fear and anxiety, insecurity and loss. Now, 7.5 years into my life with MSA, it appears my mind is failing faster than my body. My cognition is going off, my emotions are growing raw. From the day of my diagnosis, I committed to fight, to fight hard. Maybe I'm expecting too much. Maybe I'm simply too tired....

March 30, 2018

Those of you who have followed this page for a while know that little Lady the Wonder Dog was my constant companion. Sadly, today was her last. At 15 1/2, she had given all she was able to give and was struggling to be my caregiver to the very end.

Lady, the Wonderdog

It's hard to imagine a more faithful and loyal friend. She'll stay in my heart forever.

April 26, 2018

Day by day with MSA, I've learned to:

-eat lightly, simply, frequently

-exercise regularly, carefully, in various ways

-socialize often, in different settings with different people

-challenge my limits, employ neural training, take one step more than I think possible

-make each day count, whether I'm resting in bed or here at my favorite spot.

Create your own treatment plan...keep your spirit aloft.

May 18, 2018

How lucky I am to be making arrangements to visit Doctor Zoltan Mari at the Lou Ruvo Center for Brain Health in Las Vegas.

In addition to a full neuro assessment, we will be discussing Dr. Mari's presentation of dataMSA findings in Hong Kong this fall.

The Lou Ruvo Center will likely be the custodian of the dataMSA databases; however, all personal information will be redacted.

This will ensure that the data will be available to researchers for further and future analysis and disaggregation.

I cannot adequately express my gratitude to the 700+ of you who shared your experiences.

If you would like to review the survey results, please visit dataMSA.com

Cheers.

May 19, 2018

7.5 years. Now what? Well, I'm a lucky lad. Physically, I'm holding on...thanks, largely, to consistent neural training strategies.

But I feel a shift in cognition, in emotionality. I experience processing deficits, memory failure and increased impulsivity.
I get overwhelmed by life at times. Yes, depression.
What have I learned?

Stay active in all ways possible. Stimulate your mind, challenge your body. Stay social, engage yourself in projects. Find a sense of purpose. Meditate. Be mindful of your spiritual self. Be grateful, discard resentment. Seek emotional wellbeing through balance. Fight with every ounce of your being. Do what you can, then do a bit more.

Remember, acceptance is not the same as complacency. And take time to smile. Somehow, you'll feel better.

We must believe there is hope on the horizon.

dataMSA.com

We know all too well that our systems are atrophying, but did you know you can do something about some aspects of that? It's well known that everyone must keep their muscular systems exercised, including lungs, heart, and the skeletal muscular system. It's even more important for us MSA folks to do so.

To stimulate your diaphragm and expand your lung capacity, breathing exercises can be beneficial. These are best done while sitting up straight, but if that is not possible, they can be done while lying down.

Inhale steadily through the nose until the lungs are full, hold this to the count of ten (if you are able), and slowly exhale through the mouth. Repeat this three or four times at intervals throughout the day. Of course, if you feel faint, stop right away.

Physical activity is also essential for our cardio health and muscular strength retention. Even if you're bound to a bed or chair, you can exercise by rotating your ankles, lifting your legs, using a squeeze ball for your hands, using light weights for your arms, practicing head rolls for your neck, and so forth.
If you are able to do so, leg lifts or sit ups will help build your core, which may help prevent falls.

Keeping yourself in the best physical shape possible will help you adapt to the changes of MSA and increase quality of life.

I would suggest you discuss these options with your health care providers, PT/OT and neurologist(s) to reduce any risks of harm.

If you'd like more information about the techniques I employee, drop me a line. I follow studies on neuro training, redundant circuits and brain plasticity. I think it's helping, but at least it makes me feel I'm doing something positive for myself!

July 25, 2018

Most of you know for several years, I've been implementing neural training techniques to fight this rot. A few years into my diagnosis, with things deteriorating, I asked several neurologists if our MSA brains might respond similarly to interventions used to help those with traumatic brain injury. In other words, does the brain know the difference between organic and traumatic injury?

Apparently, in general, it does not.

From there, I adopted from strategies developed for TBI, adjusted for my resources and abilities. Using my training as a special-needs teacher, I developed a treatment plan for myself, with goals, activities and timelines.

Of course, the trick is sticking with it...but I find that the results have been good. I've been living with MSA for nearly 8 years....

You may learn more about my neural adventures, and 'hear' from more than 700 of our MSA colleagues worldwide, at www.dataMSA.com

July 26, 2018

Good news, everyone! A research abstract based on the survey information you shared via dataMSA.com has been approved for presentation at the International Congress of Parkinson's Disease and Movement Disorders® in Hong Kong from October 5-9, 2018!

Following the presentation, the abstract will be published in an electronic supplement to the Movement Disorders journal, online edition. Additional publication is pending.

This will allow neuro-specialists across the globe to view, analyze and disaggregate dataMSA information from the 700+ individuals who participated.

Thank you, always, for your contribution to this research. Remember, no funds are generated from this data and no private participant information is shared. Cheers.

From: Abhimanyu Mahajan
Movement Disorders Fellow at University of Cincinnati

Mr. Sydnor, thanks for connecting. I just made the poster from data collected through dataMSA and Dr. Mari will be presenting the same at the Annual MDS congress in Hong Kong in October where I'm sure it will be very well received.

September 16, 2018

Interesting, intriguing...according to the dataMSA surveys of 700 patients, nearly 20% experienced one or more head traumas. I've suffered several head injuries, many resulting in concussion, some with loss of consciousness. I've always wondered....

October 10, 2018

Good day, all! First, I extend my wishes for healing and recovery to all in the path of the Hurricane Michael, a terrible storm. Below is a link that will allow you to review all the abstracts presented at the 2018 International Congress related to MSA. Thankfully there are several, representing a wide and varied scope.

I hope you will find this information helpful; you may find specific topics to share with your health care providers.

Thank you, always.

Visit: http://www.mdsabstracts.org/?s=msa

October 16, 2018

As I wrap up my eighth year with MSA, I find I'm experiencing increased cognitive/emotional deficits...

my years of experience in Exceptional Student Education are coming in handy!

October 26, 2018

Good day, all - A tremendous thanks to all who participated in the dataMSA Survey for Multiple System Atrophy, patients present and passed, caregivers and loved ones. Your experiences have now reached tens of thousands across the globe. Our collective voices are being heard.

As you know, Zoltan Mari, MD, Section Head, Cleveland Clinic Lou Ruvo Center for Brain Health and the Center for Neurological Restoration, presented the dataMSA Survey Summary at the International Congress of Parkinson's Disease and Movement Disorders® in Hong Kong this month.

This presentation was well received and widely reviewed, rating #3 of more than 1400 abstracts shared. As of today:
MDS Abstracts Site: Most Viewed Abstracts This Month-

1) Effect of marijuana on Essential Tremor: A case report
2) Autonomic Dysfunction in Parkinson's Disease: Role of New Surrogate Markers
3) Patient Perspective in Multiple System Atrophy
4) DaTscan in clinical evaluation of Multiple System Atrophy
5) Long-term Parkinson's disease progression in PIGD and TD subtypes in the PPMI cohort

So, thanks! You have made a difference for all of us and those who may follow.

October 27, 2018

Thanks to all of you for your notes of support for dataMSA! But I must clarify, I am not a doctor. I'm a patient who wanted to learn more about the experiences of fellow MSA patients. To do so, I created the dataMSA surveys. Through you, I've learned a great deal and have been able to share your voices worldwide. But I am not an expert in any area of this illness. Just a patient looking for answers, like you. Cheers

Patient perspective in Multiple System Atrophy

Abhimanyu Mahajan, MD, MHS; Zoltan Mari, MD
Department of Neurology, Henry Ford Health System, Detroit, MI; University of Cincinnati, Cincinnati, OH
Division Chair and Director, Parkinson's & Movement Disorders Program, Cleveland Clinic Lou Ruvo Center for Brain Health, Las Vegas

Introduction

- The majority of literature on Multiple System Atrophy's (MSA) natural history comes from single center studies or region specific cohorts.

- As such, site or region independent MSA-specific patient perspectives, integral to patient-centered care, may not have been adequately captured.

Objective

To report patient and/or caregiver perspective in Multiple System Atrophy (MSA)

Methods

- Information on demographics, clinical features and management was collected as part of a patient survey made available online in March 2014.
- Data from March 2014 to January 2018, data on 852 MSA patients or caregivers was collected.
- Permission to use this information was granted by the creator of the survey (a patient with MSA) for the purpose of research.
- As it is a publically available data with no identifiable PHI, no IRB was considered necessary for its use.

Results

- While 37% of responders were MSA patients, 63% were caregivers. Males comprised 58.9% of all responders. The majority of responders were from North America with some from Asia, Africa, Europe and Australia.
- Approximately 40.2% responders reported their age of diagnosis between 51-60 years. MSA Parkinsonian subtype was the diagnosis in 27.5%, with 43.4% reporting the cerebellar subtype.
- It took greater than 2 years for 44% of patients to be given a diagnosis of MSA with consultation with 3 or more neurologists required by 57% of patients.
- Most commonly reported clinical manifestations included difficulty walking (92.3%), impaired balance (93.7%), impaired fine motor skills (80%), falls (79.1%), impaired bladder control (71.2%) and unstable blood pressure (68.5%).

Results

- Only 14% of the patients lived 8 years or more after a diagnosis of MSA, with 59% of respondents reporting respiratory infection or failure as cause of death.
- 21.8% reported that the patients donating their brain for research.

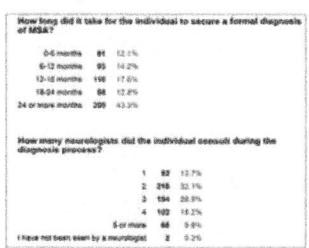

Conclusion

- This is the first time a patient-initiated, patient-organized database on MSA patient perspectives have been analyzed and reported.
- Such data is central to good patient care and patient advocacy efforts.
- Early diagnosis and symptom management is key to good quality of life in MSA patients.

Reference

Ref: Moreno MA et al. Ethics of Social Media Research: Common Concerns and Practical Considerations. Cyberpsychology, Behavior and Social Networking. 2013

Dr. Mari's presentation at the 2018 International MDS Congress

November 28, 2018

This time of year, there are countless requests for donations...including MSA.

My experiences taught me it's wise to align our resources, as we strive for efficacy. Through collaboration with other neurosystem research/education initiatives, all our boats may be lifted!

My holiday wish is that we're able to pull together....

December 3, 2018

Dean and I were discussing how fortunate I was to have been relatively young, healthy and fit when I was diagnosed.
This has allowed me to fight back in all ways possible. Of course, I had to laugh at the irony of being. 'fortunate'.
In life, all things are relative....

204

2019

January 17, 2019

Several data sources indicate that those of us who move into 8 or more years w/MSA are likely to experience increased levels of depression, cognitive impairment, memory loss, processing deficits and anxiety.

Hear, hear!

January 22, 2019

A new member of my treatment team observed that many of my symptoms align to traumatic brain injury (i.e., CTE) rather than MSA. I have always suspected that multiple severe head traumas I suffered years back may be the root of my condition.

Could my assessment from Mayo Clinic (and other specialists) be wrong? Both conditions are quite difficult to diagnose reliably. Regardless, progression and outcomes of the two are quite similar. Onward, day by day...

February 8, 2019

Good day, all- as you may know, I've been rather curious about contemporary research that links multiple head injury to degenerative neurological disease later in life. Studies indicate that such injuries can contribute to Alzheimer's disease, Parkinson's disease and, of course, chronic traumatic encephalopathy (CTE).

I contacted friend to dataMSA, Dr. Zoltan Mari, to seek his knowledge regarding any links between head injury and multiple system atrophy. His response is copied below.

Dr. Mari and Dr. Mahajan have shown great interest in the information collected through dataMSA, which represents more than 800 individuals affected by MSA. You may recall that Dr. Mari presented dataMSA findings at the 2018 International Congress of Parkinson's Disease and Movement Disorders in Hong Kong.

After the dataMSA Survey for Multiple System Atrophy closes at the end of this month (Feb2019), Dr. Mari and staff will study the results of this 5-year project, which collected patient-driven data from across the globe.

February 11, 2019

Good day, all - As I continue to explore the patient information submitted through dataMSA.com, I am personally interested in these results from a question in the dataMSA Survey for Multiple System Atrophy:

With regard to possible MSA-contributing factors, which of the following did the individual experience prior to receiving a diagnosis of MSA?

-Prior single traumatic brain injury - 4.2%

-Prior multiple traumatic brain injuries - 1.4%

-Prior single head trauma resulting in concussion - 7.9%

-Prior multiple head traumas resulting in concussion - 9%

A doctor new to my treatment group has reviewed my own history of head injuries (10+) and is exploring the possibility of chronic traumatic encephalopathy (CTE). He reports that my symptoms more closely align to CTE than later-stage MSA.

In the 8 years since I was diagnosed with MSA, a great deal of research has been completed linking multiple head injuries to progressive neuro-degenerative disease.

Mayo Clinic has this to say:

"CTE is thought to cause areas of the brain to waste away (atrophy). Injuries to the section of nerve cells that conduct electrical impulses affect communication between cells.

-It's possible that people with CTE may show signs of another neurodegenerative disease, including Alzheimer's disease, amyotrophic lateral sclerosis (ALS) — also known as Lou Gehrig's disease — Parkinson's disease or frontotemporal lobar degeneration — also known as frontotemporal dementia.

-Some of the possible signs and symptoms of CTE may include:

- Difficulty thinking (cognitive impairment)
- Impulsive behavior
- Depression or apathy
- Short-term memory loss
- Difficulty planning and carrying out tasks (executive function)
- Emotional instability
- Substance abuse
- Suicidal thoughts or behavior
- Other suspected symptoms may include:
- Irritability
- Aggression
- Speech and language difficulties
- Motor impairment, such as difficulty walking, tremor, loss of muscle movement, weakness or rigidity

- Trouble swallowing (dysphagia)
- Vision and focusing problems
- Trouble with sense of smell (olfactory abnormalities)
- Dementia

-The full list of symptoms of people with CTE at autopsy is still unknown. It is unclear what kind of symptoms, if any, it may cause. Little is known right now about how CTE progresses."

Like MSA, CTE is extremely difficult to diagnose. Mayo Clinic states: "There is currently no reliable way to diagnose CTE. A diagnosis requires evidence of degeneration of brain tissue and deposits of tau and other proteins in the brain that can be seen only upon inspection after death (autopsy). Some researchers are actively trying to find a test for CTE that can be used while people are alive. Others continue to study the brains of deceased individuals who may have had CTE

-Neurological tests include:

- Speech, language and cognition — including short- and long-term memory
- Reflexes
- Muscle tone and strength
- Ability to get up from a chair and walk across the room
- Sense of sight and hearing
- Coordination
- Balance.

-Eventually, the hope is to use a range of neuropsychological tests, brain imaging and biomarkers to diagnose CTE. In particular, imaging of amyloid and tau proteins will aid in diagnosis. CTE is a progressive, degenerative brain disease for which there is no treatment. "

I continue to search for answers...for us all.

February 21, 2019

Good day, all. According to the dataMSA Survey for Multiple System Atrophy, 6.2% of nearly 800 respondents suffered 1 or more traumatic brain injuries prior to MSA diagnosis. An additional 17.2% suffered one or more head injuries resulting in concussion prior to MSA diagnosis. No data was collected from the original survey regarding head injury after MSA diagnosis.

Thank you sincerely for helping us expand the awareness/knowledge of MSA by sharing your patient-driven experiences.

February 26, 2019

Still here at the hospital, being admitted and spending at least one night. Collapsed at about 8:15 this morning (not long after taking this pic) while exercising at the beach.
Pulse was so low paramedics could not detect it. Administered CPR briefly. I wasn't responding to verbal or physical stimulation. Thankfully, doing much better...just exhausted now. They're going to run more tests...MSA is a mystery to most.
More later...

March 2, 2019

Well, gang...you know my saying, "Do what you can, and then do a bit more"? That got me into a bit of trouble this past week (actually, a lot of trouble) so I am modifying it to read, "Do all you can, safely!"

I'm not backing off, but I am modifying my activities to ensure that I am safe. No more beach walks (too hot here, I am too vulnerable). No activities alone. Instead, more workouts at our hospital wellness center, under staff supervision. And a smart watch with fall detection and pulse rate monitor.

As MSA progresses, I must upgrade my adaptations and accommodations...so I can keep fighting!

March 7, 2019

Well, I have my smart phone, my Apple Watch, fall detection, EKG, heart rate monitor... I think I'm going to be okay.

March 25, 2019

Although the proteins present in CTE and MSA are quite dissimilar, there is data that appears to link multiple head injuries to Parkinson's Disease and ALS-adjacent neurological degenerative disease.

April 16, 2019

I think I'm able to keep going because I keep doing.... whatever I can, whenever I can. Some days find me weak, bed bound, exhausted, but I use those days to plan for stronger days. In my career, I worked with brain-injured and disabled children. I witnessed how important physical activity and socialization are to recover and maintain skills. I've applied this knowledge from the first day of my diagnosis.

I know how fortunate I was to have been diagnosed at 53, in good health and physically fit. This enabled me to push back against encroaching limitations. I then began to apply principles of neuroplasticity and brain training in hopes of engaging dormant neuro pathways to compensate for those being lost to MSA.

I was also very fortunate to have participated in a clinical trial for rifampicin, which was not approved for MSA, but may have slowed my progression.

And thanks to more than 1000 surveys shared by you on dataMSA.com, I learned so much about the disease... and about myself. Of course, there are many things I can't begin to understand, many things I can't possibly explain.

It sure helps to live here, where I can challenge myself whenever I am strong enough. I'm grateful for each new day!

April 23, 2019

Most of you know I've been using neuro training to push my limits in an attempt to slow MSA progression. I don't have any hard data to prove it works, but I can see improvement in my quality-of-life. One thing I haven't been able to overcome is chronic fatigue. I may get a few good hours in the morning, and then down I go...for hours. Zzzzz

May 6, 2019

My basic neuro eval today indicated a significant slowing of progression.... but why? More tests later this month.

May 7, 2019

Good morning, all! I feel I should add some clarification to yesterday's post - After a rather rudimentary assessment, my neurologist was surprised to find that my autonomic systems have not degenerated as one would expect. I still present motor skill deficits and declining cognition and processing abilities, as well as chronic fatigue (and a smattering of other issues).

We discussed the potential impact that a history of multiple head injuries in my youth/young adulthood may have played in my current neurological functioning. A review of past and present CT data is inconclusive.

He has prescribed a full battery of neuro-psychological testing to assess levels of functioning and will review past assessments done at Mayo Clinic at the time of my diagnosis for comparison.

I asked him if it was possible that my 'neuro-training' approach of seeking healthy neuropathways to bypass damaged/affected areas could have proven effective. He wasn't sure but couldn't rule it out.

When all the assessments are completed and reports written, they will be reviewed by the Lou Ruvo Center for Brain

Health in Las Vegas. As you may recall, the LRCBH is analyzing the raw data from the dataMSA surveys.

So, good news? Yes, it appears to be. But questions remain.

"It is a riddle, wrapped in a mystery, inside an enigma; but perhaps there is a key." Winston Churchill

More later.

May 31, 2019

Warning- this is a bit long! Many of you know my quest to identify whether the many head traumas experienced in my youth/young adulthood significantly contributed to my MSA status. I found the report below to be enlightening.

Chronic Traumatic Encephalopathy Pathology in Multiple System Atrophy © 2016 American Association of Neuropathologists, Inc.

Abstract (summarized):

Chronic traumatic encephalopathy (CTE) is a progressive neurodegenerative disorder associated with repetitive traumatic brain injury. Multiple system atrophy (MSA) is a Parkinsonian disorder that can result in repetitive falls with associated head trauma.

We hypothesized that patients with neurodegenerative disorders like MSA could develop CTE pathology. Therefore, we assessed CTE pathology in 139 MSA cases in our brain bank. Aging-related tau astrogliopathy (ARTAG) was differentiated from CTE pathology. For cases with suggestive CTE pathology, sections of basal forebrain and hippocampus were immunostained.

214

Of the 139 MSA cases, 8 (6%) had CTE pathology and 10 (8%) had ARTAG pathology. All 8 cases with CTE were male; even without a known history of contact sports or head trauma, a small subset of cases with MSA had CTE pathology.

In review of my notes, I would like to add-The generalized collection of CTE presenting symptoms include: (* = symptoms I present)

*Difficulty thinking (cognitive impairment)

*Impulsive behavior

*Depression or apathy

*Short-term memory loss

*Difficulty planning and carrying out tasks (executive function)

*Emotional instability

Substance abuse

*Suicidal thoughts or behavior

*Irritability

*Aggression

Speech and language difficulties

*Motor impairment, such as difficulty walking, tremor, loss of muscle movement, weakness or rigidity

*Trouble swallowing (dysphagia)

*Vision and focusing problems

Trouble with sense of smell (olfactory abnormalities)

Dementia

The generalized collection of MSA presenting symptoms include: (* = symptoms I present)

Rigid muscles

Difficulty bending your arms and legs

Slow movement (bradykinesia)

*Tremors (rare in MSA compared with classic Parkinson's disease)

*Problems with posture and balance

*Problems with muscle coordination (ataxia)

*Impaired movement and coordination, such as unsteady gait and loss of balance

Slurred, slow or low-volume speech (dysarthria)

*Visual disturbances, such as blurred or double vision and difficulty focusing your eyes

*Difficulty swallowing (dysphagia) or chewing

Postural (orthostatic) hypotension

Urinary and bowel dysfunction

Constipation

Loss of bladder or bowel control (incontinence)

*Sweating abnormalities

Reduced production of sweat, tears and saliva

*Heat intolerance due to reduced sweating

Impaired body temperature control, often causing cold hands or feet

*Sleep disorders

Agitated sleep due to "acting out" dreams

*Abnormal breathing at night

*Sexual dysfunction

*Inability to achieve or maintain an erection (impotence)

*Loss of libido

Cardiovascular problems

Irregular heartbeat

*Psychiatric problems

*Difficulty controlling emotions, such as laughing or crying inappropriately

I undergo a full battery of neuropsych assessments starting next week. Eight years after diagnosis, I have to wonder: am I a member of that 6%?

some days just ruffle your feathers !

June 6, 2019

After 8 years post diagnosis (based on thorough testing), my neuro-team now thinks MSA could be a secondary or co-condition to a yet unknown primary neurological condition.
That could be CTE, based on head injury history and presenting symptoms. Or not...

The tough spot we're all in is the accuracy of our diagnosis; only necropsy can supply finite answers at this point.

Progress in research is being made as I write this...meanwhile, I face more assessments. Or not...I'm pretty tired.

June 13, 2019

I keep searching for answers - Chronic traumatic encephalopathy (CTE) is likely caused by repeated head trauma; I had many in youth and young adulthood (10+, several concussions and some with loss of consciousness). The chart attached indicates CTE symptoms; I present 11 out of 14. However, my prominent MSA symptoms include:

- -anxiety/ depression
- -ataxia/balance, coordination
- -clumsiness or incoordination
- -difficulty swallowing,
- -fainting or lightheadedness due to orthostatic hypotension
- -fatigue
- -involuntary, uncontrollable sighing/gasping
- -sleep disorders
- -slowness of movement, tremor

A 2016 study sought to assess CTE pathology in 139 MSA cases in a brain bank. Of the 139 MSA cases, 8 (6%) had had tau pathology consistent with CTE.

Some MSA patients with CTE pathology had developed memory loss, behavioral changes or chronic headaches, cognitive impairments and depression. Results in the study also indicate that the threshold that triggers CTE pathology might be lower than previously thought.

July 2, 2019

Some nights, my breathing is labored; I may catch myself "gulping". Last night I had a dream that I was in respiratory distress and couldn't get help. Not good. This morning, I figured I'd better get to my place of respite and deep breathe some briny sea air! Aaaaah....

July 3, 2019

What do others affected by MSA experience? More than 1,000 survey results may be explored at dataMSA.com. Summaries of the surveys were presented at the 2018 Movement Disorder Symposium in Hong Kong by Dr. Zoltan Mari, Lou Ruvo Center for Brain Health.

Currently, neuro specialists are studying the data to identify possible trends/patterns in MSA.

Thanks to all who shared their experiences. Each individual remains confidential and no funds are generated from the surveys.

July 15, 2019

As my 9th year soon comes to a close, I am becoming more and more suspicious of my MSA diagnosis. Some of my symptoms align, others don't. And my progression is atypical.

I was diagnosed by a neuro team at our local Holy Cross Hospital, then my records were reviewed my Miami Jackson Memorial and Mayo Clinic JAX. Within 18 months, I was assessed by Mayo Clinic for inclusion in the Rifampicin trials. I was accepted and my diagnosis was reconfirmed. During the trail I underwent 2 additional full clinical assessments, including full autonomic tests. At the close of the 1-year trial, my MSA diagnosis was confirmed with poor prognosis.

At any rate, in a couple of weeks I'll undergo a full battery of assessments, the first set of comprehensive tests since the Rifampicin trial assessments. Stay tuned. I know I will!

July 21, 2019

Soooo...what do I do when I'm stuck on Bed Island? Nothing physical (heck, my eyes won't even open), but my mind is full, just the same. Aside from the dataMSA Surveys for Multiple System Atrophy: Patient Data Report (a collection of more than 1,000 surveys of MSA patient/caregiver experiences), I've put together some tales of historic fiction, Mitchell's Magical Days.

About 20 years back, I started a series of children's books about our local history in south Florida, specifically Fort Lauderdale. As a boy, I had many opportunities to sit with our very first schoolteacher, as she told tales of her life with her husband at their trading post on the New River in the late 1800s.

The protagonist of the series, Mitchell, is loosely based on a 14-year old special-needs student from my first year of teaching. Despite his many cognitive and physical challenges, Mitchell shared his love of story- telling through his incredible imagination. All these books are a tribute to this kind and gifted young man. Mitchell lost his battle for life at the age of 15. I donate all the proceeds from the Mitchell books to reading programs in our schools.

220

So, Bed Island is my spot to lie quietly and generate new adventures for Mitch. Next, he'll find himself lost in the Bermuda Triangle...Bed Island might be a safer place!

June 24, 2019

I wish someone could explain why I still have these strong mornings. They don't last long and believe me, I'm not complaining. I just don't understand it. Perhaps, the clinical reviews of my upcoming neuro assessments will hold answers...

Meanwhile, color me grateful!

August 3, 2019

Monday, I head off for updated neuro assessments. I was gathering notes and papers from my files and .... well, this is embarrassing... I was diagnosed in 2011, not 2010 as I have always stated. In Summer 2010, my GP sent me for initial testing to determine why unusual symptoms were presenting.

Not that it really makes a huge hill of beans of a difference at this point...just need to correct my mistake!

August 15, 2019

In Fall 2011, after a year or assessments, I received a working diagnosis of MSA. I was told I had about 6 years; I had just turned 54. Not long after, I was entered into the clinical trials for Rifampicin, and the diagnosis/prognosis was confirmed.

Immediately, I fought. I pushed my cognitive and physical boundaries... and I still do.

In the meantime, more research was conducted on the effects of multiple head injuries, which I have experienced.

Many symptoms of MSA and CTE are similar, many are not. Both diseases are progressive and degenerative, neither has a cure nor effective treatment.

So, where do I stand today?

- My gait is awkward, but I can walk.
- I present tremors, but I manage them.
- My ability to perspire is impaired.
- I have breathing difficulties.
- Swallowing can be challenging.
- My overall motor skills are off.
- I have bradycardia and my PB is off.
- My eyelids go wonky.
- I suffer chronic fatigue.

...and so on.

More aligned to brain repetitive injury-

- My immediate/short term memory is very poor.
- My impulsivity is very high.
- Cognitive processing is impaired.
- Attention skills are impaired.
- My thoughts easily become muddled.
- Depression is deep, meds help.
- Suicidal ideation is pervasive; therapy helps.
- Even low stress levels become debilitating.
- I suffer synesthesia-induced headaches.

...and so on.

So, I can't do what I used to. What I can still do, I can't do very well, or for very long. But I'm still here, fighting back against

MSA/CTE/etc. Take that, whatever alphabet letters are appropriate!

August 20, 2019

I have another appointment for counseling tomorrow....

I think the treatment plan is:

a) Adjust - Fight - Accept,

b) Adjust - Fight - Accept,

c) Adjust - Fight - Accept

I like the 'Fight' part the best!

August 23, 2019

This morning, I was with a friend, remembering a mutual friend and community leader we lost to MSA within 18 months of his diagnosis. I'm now wrapping up 8 years, and still able to fight most days; I begin and end each day in reflection and gratitude...

September 7, 2019

In an effort to better understand some of my atypical symptoms, I joined a couple of CTE information/support groups.

It appears that many but not all of my presenting issues are shared by the majority who were diagnosed with CTE.

In the journal article, Chronic Traumatic Encephalopathy Pathology in Multiple System Atrophy (J Neuropathol Exp Neurol. 2016 Oct), it was hypothesized that patients with neurodegenerative disorders like MSA could develop CTE pathology.

CTE pathology was assessed in 139 MSA cases as determined from the Mayo Clinic brain bank. Of that study sample, the median age at death was 66 years; 84 were men (60%); 13 patients (9%) had a family history of dementia and 13 (9%) had a family history of parkinsonism.

MSA with predominant parkinsonism was cited in 96 patients (77%) and MSA with predominant cerebellar ataxia in 29 patients (23%); it was not possible to make a designation in 14 cases due to lack of detailed clinical information about motor symptoms.

Of that total MSA sample, (6%) of the cases had tau pathology consistent with CTE. In a similar study, Ling et al. (2015) reported CTE pathology in a variety of neurodegenerative diseases in the University College London brain bank, including multiple system atrophy (MSA).

I'm still searching for a better understanding of the connections between degenerative neurological diseases...although for me living day by day, it makes little difference.

September 10, 2019

I pushed myself to go to the wellness/fitness center this morning...I'm glad I did. The staff understands my struggle with MSA and are supportive!

October 1, 2019

I continue to explore how past head injuries have affected my condition...one study indicates 6% of CTE patients are found to have MSA. I present a hybrid of the two.

October 3, 2019

I struggled to balance my will against my ability, my hope against my reality. I prefer action over apathy....

October 8, 2019

I find all of this so interesting, especially because I have always suspected I was misdiagnosed or should have a dual diagnosis, with consideration given to my history of head injury. I'll continue to search for clarity... Bill

---

-Massachusetts Medical Society, 2019:

"A recent study showed that many patients diagnosed clinically with multiple system atrophy (MSA) have other conditions on autopsy. Researchers examined the records of 203 patients with a diagnosis of MSA. Only 78.8% of the patients were correctly diagnosed and had pathologically confirmed MSA."

-The International Parkinson and Movement Disorder Society (MDS), 2018:

"The median time from the presentation of the initial symptom to combined motor and autonomic dysfunction in MSA (probable MSA) is 2 years but ranges from 1 to 19 years. Therefore, many patients with MSA who present isolated autonomic failure, parkinsonism, or cerebellar ataxia during the early phase of illness will not be diagnosed as "possible" or "probable" based on the current diagnostic criteria.

In addition, the high positive predictive value (86-100%) of MSA patients who meet the "probable" criteria was contradicted by Koga et al. showing that 38% of such cases changed the final diagnosis at autopsy. The presence of autonomic failure and cerebellar ataxia were the leading causes of misdiagnosis of dementia with Lewy bodies (DLB) and progressive supranuclear palsy (PSP), respectively. On the other hand, symptoms of DLB and PSP such as dementia, hallucinations, and vertical gaze palsy may be observed in MSA patients. Consequently, a revision of the second consensus criteria for the early and clinically definitive diagnosis of MSA is urgently needed."

October 27, 2019

I fight to stay physically active and strong. It can be a real struggle, but I know it's what's keeping me going. My motto has always been, "Do what you can, when you can. Then try to do a bit more." (Within safe parameters, of course.)  Research continues to reinforce the importance of exercise for neurological health. Nike got it right: Just do it!

October 31, 2019

Well, I've made a decision. I want no more testing, no more assessments, no more just-because doctor visits, no more shot-in-the-dark explanations. No more prodding and poking and scanning and tests, no more "might be" or "could be"

226

or "should be" prognoses, no more, "There's nothing we can do, we'll see you in 6 months."

I'm tired of being the "patient".

For several years, I've regularly posted my day to day experiences. For more than 5 years, I've collected, shared and reviewed patient information on dataMSA.com - that information is in the hands of very capable researchers at the Lou Ruvo Center for Brain Health.

I've read and studied and spoken with neurologists from all over. Now it's time to step aside.

So, I'm signing off for a while - maybe a long while- to focus on the non-MSA side of my being; to relish what I have while I have it; to celebrate the joy of just being, regardless of the uncertainty ahead.

Thank you, my friends, for being at my side throughout. I hope you, too, will take time to step off the MSA treadmill for a bit. I hope we each can find a level of purpose and identity separate and apart from our diagnosis, a level of comfort in just being - whatever that may look like.

So, "Cheers, until we meet again down the road!"

Seek the strength
to accept the things
you cannot change,
things you cannot
begin to understand.

dataMSA.com

Onward

In recent years, I often question the accuracy of my diagnosis. I underwent extensive and thorough assessments at the Mayo Clinic prior to and during the NIH clinical trial for Rifampin. The outcomes of those assessments, and records reviews by other neurological facilities strongly indicated multiple system atrophy. I carried that working diagnosis into the years ahead.

The prognosis was poor, and Dean and I pondered the many decisions. I seriously considered cashing out my school board retirement so we could explore a bit of the world while I was still able. Instead, we decided to hunker down and adjust to what lie ahead.

It's a good thing I didn't spend my retirement funds in those early years; I'd be in a very bad position if I had. At this point, I've outlived my prognosis by approximately 2 years and I'm still going.

My primary care doctor, whose father died from MSA complications, still thinks that MSA is the primary presenting condition. My neurologist, who referred me to Mayo Clinic back in 2011, isn't sure. He isn't ready to withdraw or change my diagnosis, but he would like more assessment to rule out other possibilities.

There remains the possibility that the many head injuries I suffered in youth and young adulthood (and some from falls, later on) have created neurological damage. Although I present symptoms of CTE (chronic traumatic encephalopathy), I also present symptoms atypical and more aligned to MSA. Of course, neither can be formally diagnosed until necropsy. I'll never know, will I?

Then there is the consideration that the 1-year trial of Rifampin had a positive effect on my progression. The findings of the trail deemed to be ineffective as a treatment for MSA. But what if…?

At age 54, when I was diagnosed, I was in good physical condition. I was a nondrinker and non-smoker. I was physically and intellectually active, trim. However, by my 4th year post diagnosis, I was in bed 3 days out of 7 for a full 24 hours a day. During these times, I was nearly immobile. When I could walk, I required a cane. Doctors suggested I take it easy because I was experiencing falls that sometimes resulted in injury.

One day, after having spent 70+ hours on Bed Island, I felt a tinge of inspiration. I questioned the doctor's advice to 'take it easy'. I could readily see that I was deteriorating fast and I was idly allowing my life to slide away from me.

I began to understand that if I stood any chance of improving the quality of my life, I needed to fight. I instructed Dean to sit me up and allow my feet to touch the floor. From there, I struggled to stand. Bit by bit, day by day, I pushed myself in a stumble-legged walk from my bed to a chair, from the chair to the sofa, from the sofa back to bed. Whenever I could, I pushed a little harder.

I struggled, I cried, I grew angry at my failures. After about a year, I began to see results. I ditched my walker and donated my wheelchair. I worked to become less reliant on my cane and exercised at any level I could as often as I could.

I still I found myself stuck on Bed Island, but I was marooned less and less for fewer hours, fewer days. I also created ways to challenge my cognitive abilities. Reading was still difficult, but I kept at it.

I had created dataMSA in 2014 to learn the experiences of others in the same boat as me. Since my MSA diagnosis, I had refused any medication; I knew exactly what skills I needed to work on because none of them were blunted. As I had learned as a teacher for students with special needs, I created a treatment plan for myself with goals, objectives and timelines. Easy tasks at first, growing progressively more difficult with time.

As I write this, I find myself stronger in all ways. My core strength from exercise helps me prevent falls or to at least fall more safely. I still exercise nearly daily in whatever way I can, even in bed. When I'm able, I attend my hospital's wellness center, where a Parkinson's expert helps me with a variety of activities. Overheating remains a high risk, I must be careful.

My stamina remains very low. I may get only a few hours of strength in the morning, although I still have totally bedridden days, about 1 per every 10. Whenever I become weak or exhausted, my breathing becomes labored, my eyes won't track, my eyelids won't open properly. I experience severe drops in blood pressure (hypotension), I remain impotent (I have tried meds with no effect), and I have some toileting issues.

I have been hospitalized a few times for bradycardia (low heart rate) and was prepared to receive pacemaker prior to the 2020 COVID-19 pandemic. The procedure was delayed and while awaiting word, my insurance company announced that my cardiologist and hospital would no longer be in my coverage.

Of course, my abilities are a fraction of what they were at diagnosis. I need assistance for many daily activities, but my quality of life is far better, and my outlook has improved. So, am I an atypical MSA patient? My doctors think so, but they are quick to remind me that I may deteriorate quickly at some unknown point.

I live my life the way we all should, grateful each and every day. I'm still here, and I plan to be for a while. But for now it's time for some rest. Thank you for allowing me to share my journey through this neuro rot. *Bill.*

For more information about the

dataMSA Surveys for Multiple System Atrophy,

visit www.dataMSA.com or contact dataMSA@yahoo.com

Printed in Great Britain
by Amazon